THE SCRIPTS
THE TOMB OF THE CYBERMEN
GERRY DAVIS and KIT PEDLER

EDITED BY JOHN McELROY

TITAN BOOKS
LONDON

DOCTOR WHO *THE SCRIPTS*: THE TOMB OF THE CYBERMEN
ISBN 1 85286 146 0

Published by
Titan Books Ltd
58 St Giles High St
London WC2H 8LH

First edition August 1989
10 9 8 7 6 5 4 3 2 1

By arrangement with BBC Books, a division of BBC Enterprises Ltd

Typeset by Photoprint, Torquay, Devon.
Printed and bound in Great Britain by Cox and Wyman Ltd, Reading,
Berkshire

CONTENTS

INTRODUCTION

The first *Doctor Who* Script Book, *The Tribe of Gum*, has proved very popular both with long-term fans of the programme as well as with more recent devotees, many of whom weren't even born when *The Tribe of Gum* was first transmitted.

In the first book, I invited people to write in with their opinions and suggestions for future books. Many people have done so and, although it has not been possible to answer every letter, we have taken note of each and every idea submitted.

Several ideas have not been possible to implement. A common request was for photographs from the relevant story to be included in each book. This would be impractical for several reasons. Firstly, the additional cost of printing photographs and making clearance payments to the artistes in them would increase considerably the cost of each book and, secondly, there are simply not enough photographs in existence from many of the early black and white stories. This being the case, we would inevitably be forced to publish the scripts of stories from which sufficient photographs existed, rather than using the far more important criterion of choosing the best scripts.

Another common suggestion was for us to include

camera directions and lighting directions. We have carefully considered this but we feel that, if we were to include these as well as the scene descriptions, the resulting text would become very hard to read. As publishers we are bound to consider both the casual reader, as well as the committed fan, when making these decisions.

Many people have asked how we go about choosing which scripts we will publish. *The Tribe of Gum* was an obvious choice since it was the very first story. The book that you are reading, *The Tomb of the Cybermen*, was chosen because tragically it no longer exists in the BBC's archives, and because it is thought by many to be one of the all-time great *Doctor Who* stories. A lot of readers assumed that, since we had started at the very beginning, we would continue to publish the stories in the order in which they were transmitted. Again, this was deemed impracticable. It would mean that people who are interested in the more recent stories would have to wait years before any of them were published. It is our intention to publish scripts from all of the Doctor's incarnations, although there will probably be a bias towards older stories.

When the format of the Script Books was first devised, it was agreed that we should use the actual transmitted version. As I have already said, *The Tomb of the Cybermen* is one of the 'lost' stories, of which the BBC no longer has a copy on videotape. Fortunately the BBC's script library does keep a copy of each and every *Doctor Who* script, but this is very often not a *verbatim* account of what was actually said on screen. Most often it is the 'Camera' script, which is the final version of the script that is used while recording takes place. Some actors, however, frequently deliver the gist of their lines rather than exactly what is printed in the script. Patrick Troughton, who played the Second Doctor, admitted on several occasions that he had a reputation for doing just this, to the delight of viewers who benefited from a delivery which came more from the heart rather than from the scripted page, but often to the frustration of other actors who were left waiting for a particular cue word that never came!

I have had access to an audio tape of *Tomb of the Cybermen*, which has ensured that the actual dialogue used in the Script Book is accurate, but I have had to rely on the combined memories of several Doctor Who 'experts', when giving details of several non-verbal scenes. Inevitably, after some twenty-three years, there are slight differences in the way that certain scenes are remembered but I believe that we have got as close as possible to a completely accurate reconstruction of this memorable story.

For some years, the BBC has been trying to track down all of the 'lost' episodes of *Doctor Who*. They have had some success with this but, at the time of writing, they are still on the look-out for some 114 episodes. Reels of film have been found in cupboards at the BBC, in Church halls, and even at a car boot sale! Indeed, it is possible that someone reading this book has an almost-forgotten film-can gathering dust in their attic, that might contain another 'long-lost classic': if so, please let us know. We will arrange for it to be returned to the BBC, so that, one day, it might be viewed again by a wider audience.

As some of you may know, consecutive episodes of any *Doctor Who* story have always featured an overlap, in the form of a reprise of the previous episode's last moments, leading up to the traditional 'cliff-hanger' ending. In the earliest days of the programme, when episodes were recorded live, this meant that the actors physically repeated the reprise at the start of each episode. After a while, however, once recording techniques had advanced enough to allow easier editing of episodes, this practice gradually ceased and the already-recorded episode end was simply added to the beginning of the next. Such was the case when *Tomb of the Cybermen* was recorded. However, despite the fact that this means a repetition at the start of episodes two, three and four, which it could be argued tends to break up the narrative of the story, I am strongly in favour of leaving them in. In doing so, each chapter remains an accurate and complete record of a particular episode. If you have any strong views on this practice, either in favour or against, then please let us know.

In doing research for this book, Gerry Davis very kindly consented to being interviewed at his home in Venice, California. The interview took place shortly before Christmas 1988. I am indebted to Gerry for his kind hospitality and, indeed, for sharing memories of his association with the world of *Doctor Who*. We have decided not to include a complete interview in this book, but have liberally used Gerry's comments throughout the Background section.

John McElroy, July 1989.

During the first three years of *Doctor Who* until 1965 the Daleks reigned supreme as the monsters viewers most loved to hate, capturing the imagination of both young and old alike. Despite several attempts to duplicate this success with such creatures as the Voord, the Zarbi and the Mechanoids, nothing came close. Nothing, that is, until the very last William Hartnell story, *The Tenth Planet*, which was to introduce the only serious challenger to the Daleks' crown — the Cybermen.

The end of the fourth season of *Doctor Who* broadcasts saw the last Dalek story for some time. Their creator, Terry Nation, had withdrawn the rights so that he could try to interest one of the American TV networks in a series featuring the 'animated pepper pots', as the Daleks were once dubbed. Despite initial interest, sadly nothing came of this.

Meanwhile, the new *Doctor Who* production team, producer Peter Bryant and Script Editor Victor Pemberton, looked towards another era of monsters with whom the Doctor might do battle. Since the Daleks were no longer available, the Cybermen were the obvious choice.

The first Cyberman story, *The Tenth Planet*, shown previously in October 1966, had caused a renewed burst of popularity for *Doctor Who* and had reversed the trend of the programme's dwindling audience figures. The story had been an unqualified success, and in a move still unusual for the series, an enemy returned after just three stories, in *The Moonbase*. This story increased the popularity of the programme and the cybernetic creatures still further, and there was to be a gap of only three more stories before they reappeared, in *The Tomb of the Cybermen*.

For writers Davis and Pedler *The Tomb of the Cybermen* was a departure from the style they had used for their first two Cybermen stories. *The Tenth Planet* idea had grown from the theme of astronauts becoming marooned in space. *The Moonbase* grew from the slightly more futuristic idea of weather control by a gravity machine on the Moon. *The Tomb of the Cybermen*, however, had no basis in factual science and took the team into a new genre, one where they felt they would be freer to use their imaginations.

The original concept for the story was that, for an unspecified reason (following a presumably calamitous defeat), the Cybermen had retreated to their Tomb. As master logicians, however, they had predicted and prepared for this eventuality, and their 'secret weapon' was that they could be reactivated at some time in the future. As Gerry Davis recounts, 'We had them more or less frozen behind membranes, curled up in foetal positions, rather like bees in a honeycomb . . . gradually breaking out.' He and Pedler also had in mind a series of endless tunnels again rather like a honeycomb, with a main control room above.

Although Davis and Pedler had not given too much thought as to precisely why, in the first place, the Cybermen had retired to the Tombs, their main idea for this story was that there had been laid a trap, designated to operate only after beings of a certain level of intelligence located the entrance to the Tombs. As Gerry Davis describes, 'At the time, there was a lot of interest in Erich Von Däniken investigating where spacemen could have landed. The idea was that spacemen in prehistory had perhaps left clues which we would find out about when *we* had advanced to a sufficient stage. This was basically the idea behind the Tombs. They only got inside because of their knowledge – primitive people could not get in. The Cybermen could then use the intelligent people. That was the theme, the trap . . .'

The team did not attempt to fit the story into any strict, overall chronology of the Cybermen. They felt that the less told about any subject the easier it would be to write about in the future. Gerry Davis still believes this, 'I loathe and detest people who produce these elaborate histories. As a writer you have to memorise this but it's gobbledegook. Yes, *Doctor Who*'s evolved, but if you write for *Doctor Who* you're restricted. My idea is to have a Doctor whom nobody knows . . . where he came from etc. You have a blank sheet of paper.'

Although Gerry Davis is best known nowadays as a writer, he had previously tried his hand at acting, and he has frequently called on this experience to shape his writing. While in Montreal playing the part of the evil Jonathan in *Arsenic and Old Lace*, he had decided that when Jonathan appeared from behind some curtains it should be sudden, rather than a slow appearance. This proved very popular with the audiences, who gasped at this point in every performance. Davis kept this in mind while writing *The Tomb of the Cybermen* and this shock appearance is used to best effect at the end of episode one in the weapons testing room when the first figure of a Cyberman appears.

As with their previous collaborations, Pedler and Davis wrote stories that required few sets. Gerry Davis explains,

'One of the things I always used to do in plotting out *Doctor Who* was to utilise the money in one, large set. I am a great believer in the unity of drama. You can get the drama in one set and people get used to it, then suddenly you can produce the surprise! Always jumping into something fresh doesn't pay off in that type of drama.' Davis liked claustrophobic stories and, because of the 'hidden menace' aspect, the Cybermen never came on in the first episode.

The energies which they brought to bear on their scripting passed under the direction of the *Doctor Who* Script Editor, Victor Pemberton, who recalls that he had little trouble with the writing team of Gerry Davis and Kit Pedler. He describes the two as 'a marvelous duo . . . Kit was a great technical expert and Gerry the dramatist.' In their several meetings together, Victor Pemberton's main input was to emphasize the sinister, spooky aspect of the story, particularly the Cybermen's Tomb itself. He imagined the Tombs to be a variation on the Pharoah's tomb, but with transparent fronts rather than solid stone. For Pemberton this story 'had all the elements of a creepy *Doctor Who* story . . . a story with everything leading on from one thing to another'.

The Tomb of the Cybermen also saw the introduction of the Cybermats. This was for two reasons. Davis and Pedler thought that the Cybermen should have some ancillary means of defence and that, as well, the Cybermats themselves might be a good marketing idea. The success of the Daleks in the area of merchandising had not been lost on the writers, who, of course, stood to reap the benefits of any such exploitation. Little interest was shown in this direction, though the Cybermats still appeared in two further stories.

As for the Cybermen themselves, Davis and Pedler did not see them as essentially evil. As Gerry Davis explains,

'That was our belief, that most evil is done by people who act out of logic, without ethics, without tempering it. There's nothing more dangerous, nothing more ruthless, than the person who acts for the best motives. A cold, clinical sort of way of approaching things. There are very few people who set out to do bad in this world. Hitler justified himself all the way in a very loud voice. He was righting the wrongs.'

The Tomb of the Cybermen proved to be one of the most talked about stories of its time, particularly the controversy surrounding the foam which issued from dying Cybermen. Many viewers found this repugnant, labelling it too shocking for a children's programme. Others valued the way it revealed a residual, almost human frailty remaining beneath the Cybermen's mechanical exteriors. The story's dark and moody sets, superb direction and the menacing Cybermen all came together to provide a story worthy of the label 'classic'.

* * *

Location filming for *Tomb* took place in the summer of 1967 at the Gerrard's Cross gravel quarry in Hertfordshire. Sequences shot there were of the exterior of the Cyber City in episode one. Filming also took place at the Ealing Film Studios for the Tombs themselves. All the scenes of the Cybermen being revived were filmed there, enabling the Director to reverse the film when the Cybermen are revived and then frozen again, in episode two. The Tombs' lower cells were then rebuilt in the television studio, to allow video-taping of the rest of the story.

Some of the Cybermats were radio controlled, which gave endless fun for the production crew in the studio except when, during recording, the electronics in the television studio caused interference and the Cybermats shot off in totally unexpected directions!

Recording took place on Saturday 1st, 15th, 22nd July 1967 all in Studio D Lime Grove. Recording for each episode started at 20.30 and finished at 21.45.

Although video tape editing techniques were by no means in their infancy by 1967, the episodes were still recorded in scene order, with as few breaks as possible. In episode two and three there is only one break, for the actors to reposition themselves. In episode four the breaks total six in all, mainly for repositioning of shots.

No music was specially composed for the story, all of it coming from stock music for films and television. In *The Tenth Planet* the orchestral track *Space Adventure*, by Martin Slavin, had been used as the 'Cyber-theme'. This was also used in *The Moonbase* and again in *The Tomb of the Cybermen*. Other more electronic stock tracks were also used.

The sets were as follows:

Film (on location)
  Cyber City Exterior/Doorway
Film (at Ealing)
  Tomb cells, full set
Videotape (Studio)
  TARDIS interior
  Cyber Main Control Room
  Recharging Room
  Testing Room.
  Tomb Passage
  Tomb cells, lower part
  Ladder area from Tombs to Control Room

MAIN CAST

The Doctor .... Patrick Troughton
Jamie McCrimmon ...... Frazer Hines
Victoria Waterfield ..... Deborah Watling
Toberman .... Roy Stewart
Professor Parry .... Aubrey Richards
John Viner .... Cyril Shaps (Episodes 1,2)
Jim Callum .... Clive Merrison (Episodes 1,3,4)
Kaftan .... Shirley Cooklin*
Captain Hopper .... George Roubicek
Eric Klieg .... George Pastell
Ted Rogers .... Alan Johns (Episode 1)
Peter Haydon .... Bernard Holley (Episodes 1,2)
Cyberman Controller .... Michael Kilgarriff
                                       (Episodes 2,3,4)

SUPPORTING CAST

Crewman .... Ray Grover (Episode 1)
Man in Bio-Projector ... Frankie Dunn (Episodes 1,4)
Cybermen .... Hans De Vries (Episodes 2,3,4)

* Shirley Cooklin was the producer Peter Bryant's wife.

Tony Harwood (Episodes 2,3,4)
John Hogan (Episodes 2,3,4)
Richard Kerley (Episodes 2,3,4)
Ronald Lee (Episodes 2,3,4)
Charles Pemberton
               (Episodes 2,3,4)
Kenneth Seeger (Episodes 2,3,4)
Reg Whitehead (Episodes 2,3,4)
Cybermen Voices .... Peter Hawkins (Episodes 2,3,4)

Story Code: MM

Story Title: The Tomb of The Cybermen

Authors: Kit Pedler and Gerry Davis

Number of Episodes: Four

Episode One

Duration .... 23'58"
Recorded .... 1st July 1967
Transmitted .... 2nd September 1967, at 17:49:41

Episode Two

Duration .... 24'44"
Recorded .... 8th July 1967
Transmitted .... 9th September 1967, at 17:50:08

Episode Three

Duration .... 24'14"
Recorded .... 15th July 1967
Transmitted .... 16th September 1967, at 17:50:00

Episode Four

Duration .... 23'22"
Recorded .... 22nd July 1967
Transmitted .... 23rd September 1967, at 17:50:00

Note that the practice of giving individual episodes on-screen titles, rather than giving overall story titles, had been discontinued by the time that this story was made (*The Gunfighters*, in 1966, being the last story to feature them).

This story was never repeated in the UK and, sadly, does not exist in the BBC archives.

Producer	Peter Bryant
Director	Morris Barry
Designer	Martin Johnson
Script Editor	Victor Pemberton
Production Assistant	Snowy Lidiard White
Assistant	Pat Harrington
Assistant Floor Managers	Catherine Sykes (Episodes 1,2,3)
	Sue Willis (Episode 4)
Floor Assistant	Bob Hains
Vision Mixer	Ian Easterbrook
Visual Effects	Michealjohn Harris
	Peter Day
Costume Supervisors	Sandra Reid (Episodes 1 & 2)
	Dorothea Wallace (Episodes 3 & 4)
Make-Up Supervisor	Gillian James
T.M.1	Graham Sothcott
T.M.2	Ray Hider
Sound Supervisor	Brian Hiles
Grams. Operator	Laurie Taylor
Film Cameraman	Peter Hamilton

Film Editor	Aman Martin
Crew	Number Eighteen Crew
Title Music by	Ron Grainer
Title Music realised by	Delia Derbyshire

1. THE *TARDIS* CONTROL ROOM.

THE DOCTOR: There we are . . . well, what do you think?

VICTORIA: I don't know . . . I can't believe it . . . it's so big. Where are we?

THE DOCTOR: Well, it's the TARDIS. It's my home. At least it has been for a considerable number of years.

VICTORIA: What are all these knobs?

DOCTOR: What these? Instruments.

(THE DOCTOR *demonstrates, and the* TARDIS' *power hum starts up.*)

JAMIE: These are for controlling our flight.

VICTORIA: Flight?

JAMIE: Well yes. You see we travel around in here, through Time and Space.

(VICTORIA *laughs.*)

THE DOCTOR: Oh, no, no, no, no. Don't laugh, it's true. Your father and Maxtible were working on the same problem but I have . . . er . . . perfected a . . . a rather special model . . . which enables me to travel through the universe of Time.

VICTORIA: How can you . . . I mean . . . if what you say is true, you must be . . . er, well . . . how old?

THE DOCTOR: Well if we count in Earth terms, I suppose I must be about four hundred . . . yes about 450 years old. Yes . . . well . . . quite . . .

(THE DOCTOR *tries to change the subject.*)

Now, I think that Victoria might find that dress a little impracticable if she's going to join us in our adventures. Jamie, show her where she can find some new ones, will you?

JAMIE: Aye, right. This way Victoria.

(*As* JAMIE *is about to show* VICTORIA *out of the control room,* THE DOCTOR *begins the take-off procedure.* JAMIE *pauses and goes back over to* THE DOCTOR.)

JAMIE: Try to give us a smooth take-off, Doctor. We don't want to frighten her.

THE DOCTOR: A smooth take-off? A smooth take-off! What a nerve!

(*The* TARDIS *dematerialises.*)

2. THE PLANET TELOS.

(*The head of a man can be seen peering over the top of a group of rocks. From behind him, hidden from view, comes a shout.*)

PARRY: Hey! Toberman – get that big head down.

(TOBERMAN *does not react.*)

What's the matter with you – have you gone mad?

(TOBERMAN *has been looking over the top of a cliff. He starts to descend towards the rest of the group. He is a giant of a man.*)

VINER: The fool! Doesn't he realise the danger he's in? It's nothing to laugh at – none of us knows what's going to happen when we press that thing – especially in this rarefied atmosphere.

PARRY: All right, Viner, no need to get excited.

(*He turns to a dark-haired, Middle-Eastern woman, who speaks with an almost aristocratic air.*)

Can't you keep your servant under control?

KAFTAN: If I wish, I can.

HOPPER: Hurry it up will you, Rogers. I don't know what you think you're going to find anyway.

PARRY: According to the map reference, that should be the entrance to the city of Telos.

HOPPER: I hope you're right 'cos I want to get out of here.

KLIEG: Let me remind you, Mr. Hopper, that you are being more than well paid for your part in this expedition.

(ROGERS *and another crewman appear.*)

HOPPER: Oh, big deal.

ROGERS: Sorry, we had to make it a pretty big one.

(*The group moves off up the hill and crouches down behind a rock.*)

PARRY: All right let's get on with it – we've wasted enough time . . . Stand by. Everybody down.

(*There is an explosion and the cliff-face disintegrates. As the rock-fall subsides, the group stands up and moves forward.*)

HOPPER: Well, there you go – you blast yourself one lump of rock and all you've got's another.

(*More rocks fall aside.*)

ROGERS: No, wait a minute. Look!

(*As the dust settles, a pair of metallic doors can be seen, either side of which is a crude representation of the full figure of a Cyberman!*)

HOPPER: Man, you just blew yourself a pair of doors.

(*They all clap and cheer.*)

PARRY: Well, come on. What are we waiting for?

(*The group starts climbing up the cliff-side towards the doors. As they reach them,* KAFTAN *steps forward and turns to address the group.*)

KAFTAN: Fifty pounds for the first man to open the doors.

PARRY: Miss Kaftan, I must remind you that I am the leader of . . .

(*As he talks, a crewman comes forward to open the doors and, as he grasps them, he falls to the ground, electrocuted. There is a moment's pause, and then the group rushes forward.*)

KLIEG: What happened?

PARRY: I don't know.

           (HOPPER *feels the stricken man's heart
           for signs of life.*)

HOPPER: Well, one thing for sure. He's not going to
           collect fifty pounds, from you or anybody
           else!

KLIEG: Quiet. Quiet a minute!

           (*The familiar sound of the* TARDIS
           *materialisation can be heard some-
           where nearby.*)

KAFTAN: What's that?

HAYDON: Sounded like an engine.

           (*Pause.*)

VINER: Something came down over there – behind
           that rock.

           (HOPPER *rises, drawing a gun.*)

HOPPER: Okay, Viner, slow down. I'll take care of
           this.

           (*They all scatter.* HOPPER *shouts to*
           CALLUM.)

           Jim!

CALLUM: O.K. I got it.

(CALLUM _draws his gun._ ROGERS, CALLUM, HOPPER _and_ HAYDON _all crouch down either side of a cleft in the rock._ THE DOCTOR, VICTORIA _and_ JAMIE _approach. As they get close,_ HOPPER _rises from his hiding position._)

HOPPER: Hold it right there, friend.

(THE DOCTOR _raises his hands._)

THE DOCTOR: If you put it like that, I certainly will.

VINER: Did you hear that, Professor? English!

PARRY: Yes. All right, Hopper.

THE DOCTOR: Thank you.

PARRY: Who are you and where do you come from?

HOPPER: And you'd better have a good story.

JAMIE: Maybe you'll not get one.

HOPPER: Listen fellow, we're not playing games.

VINER: You'd better listen to him.

(THE DOCTOR _spots the dead crewman._)

THE DOCTOR: Now what's been happening over here?

KLIEG: He was killed the moment you made your appearance.

THE DOCTOR: Ah, and you think we did it. Oh no. I can assure you we had nothing to do with the death of this man. He appears to have been . . . electrocuted.

(THE DOCTOR *looks at the large metal doors.*)

Trying to open these doors, perhaps?

ROGERS: He seems to know all the answers.

HOPPER: A wise guy.

VINER: I think this fellow must be a member of a rival expedition.

THE DOCTOR: Expedition?

PARRY: We've tried to keep it secret – unsuccessfully, it now appears.

VINER: Look at him. Archaeologist written all over him.

(THE DOCTOR *smiles and looks down at his clothes.*)

THE DOCTOR: Really, does it show?

VINER: There – you see. It's impossible to keep a secret in the scientific world.

VICTORIA: Doctor, what do you mean . . .

JAMIE: Tell 'em Doctor. Go on, tell them.

THE DOCTOR: No, not until they tell us the purpose of their expedition.

PARRY: This is an archaeological expedition. We are searching the Universe for the last remains of the Cybermen.

JAMIE: Cybermen? You mean to say they came from here?

PARRY: But of course. Telos was their home.

(*He points to the doors.*)

This is the entrance to their city.

VINER: We know they died out many centuries ago. What we don't know is *why* they died out.

(HOPPER, CALLUM *and* ROGERS *have been bending over the body of the dead crew-member.* HOPPER *comes up to* PARRY.)

HOPPER: Callum, Rogers!

CALLUM: Yeah?

(HOPPER *points to the body.*)

HOPPER: Take him back to the rocket. I'll be with you in a minute.

CALLUM: Yeah, OK.

HOPPER: Well that's that. Are you coming back to the rocket with me, Professor?

PARRY: What for?

HOPPER: You're not going on with this are you? Look I don't know if these people had anything to do with it or not, but one of my men has just been killed. You're not paying that kind of money.

PARRY: Yes, I suppose that's quite true.

HOPPER: Well, you think it over.

(*He looks at the crew-members.*)

Come on. Let's go.

(CALLUM *and* ROGERS *pick up the body of the dead crew-member and walk away with* HOPPER.)

We'll wait for you back at the ship.

(PARRY *nods.* THE DOCTOR *goes up to examine the doors.*)

THE DOCTOR: The problem, I take it, is to open these doors – right?

KLIEG: Hah . . . brilliant!

PARRY: That is the problem.

KLIEG: And we would prefer it if you returned to wherever you came from.

JAMIE: Oh, not very friendly are they, Doctor?

VICTORIA: Yes, do as he says.

THE DOCTOR: I'm afraid that became impossible the moment that name was mentioned.

VICTORIA: What name?

THE DOCTOR: Cybermen!

VICTORIA: Cybermen? What are they?

VINER: I knew they were here on the same quest.

PARRY: No one would come here for any other reason.

THE DOCTOR: We must stay.

JAMIE: Oh, Doctor!

VICTORIA: Oh, must we?

(*She points to one of the Cyberman motifs over the door.*)

I don't like the look of those things at all.

THE DOCTOR: We shall stay and help you with your search.

KLIEG: Perhaps we don't want your help.

THE DOCTOR: That's just it – you so obviously do. Now I am sure we can agree. I can open those doors for you.

KLIEG: This is *our* problem . . . and I suggest you take this ridiculous expedition of yours off this planet!

JAMIE: It seems to me we have as much right here as you have.

PARRY: Of course you have. Mr. Klieg, must I remind you again that you do not speak for this expedition. I am its leader. You and Miss Kaftan are only here on sufferance.

KLIEG: Thank you! And whose money is paying for the hire of that rocket?

KAFTAN: Mine.

PARRY: I though I made it quite clear that your financial support did not entitle you to a say in the running of this expedition.

> (PARRY *and* KLIEG *glare at each other.* KAFTAN, *who has been sitting in the background with the huge* TOBERMAN *standing behind her, now rises and comes forward.*)

KAFTAN: Of course – it was quite clear.

> (*She turns to* KLIEG.)

Was it not Eric?

> (KLIEG *looks at her and recovers himself.*)

KLIEG: Of course – no one questions your leadership.

THE DOCTOR: Ah good, that's all settled! And now we shall open these doors.

> (*He takes out a small pocket instrument with a dial. It clicks magnetically onto the door handle. He studies the dial then, with a sly grin, deliberately grasps the handle.*)

PARRY: Well, careful man!

HAYDON: Hey! Look out!

VICTORIA: Doctor!

> (THE DOCTOR *pauses, enjoying the sensation he is causing.*)

THE DOCTOR: It's perfectly safe now.

(*He grips the handles and exerts his strength on the doors. They do not budge.*)

VINER: You'll be killed, man.

(*He timidly puts a hand out to drag* THE DOCTOR *away.*)

HAYDON: No! Don't touch him.

(VINER *withdraws his hand.* THE DOCTOR *heaves at the doors. They remain set fast. He pauses for breath.*)

THE DOCTOR: I'm afraid it's beyond my strength.

(JAMIE *steps forward.*)

JAMIE: Let me, Doctor.

THE DOCTOR: Certainly Jamie.

(THE DOCTOR *smiles and steps aside.* JAMIE *takes the handle, and squares his shoulders. He heaves; nothing happens. He heaves again, the strain showing on his face. He realises that he cannot shift the door.*)

JAMIE: Aye, well I've not had much exercise lately.

THE DOCTOR: Quite, I think here . . .

(*He indicates* TOBERMAN.)

. . . is a gentleman who could open these doors for us.

KAFTAN: He is my servant. I will not have him risk his life.

PARRY: Surely it was just for such a contingency as this that you insisted we bring him with us?

(KAFTAN *stiffens, glaring at* PARRY.)

THE DOCTOR: Oh, there is no danger now. Unless of course he is afraid?

(TOBERMAN *steps forward, looking menacing.*)

No, no, he's not afraid.

(THE DOCTOR *stands aside from the doors.* TOBERMAN *grasps the handle and exerts all his strength. For a moment nothing happens. Then the doors start to swing outwards.* TOBERMAN *stands back.* THE DOCTOR *looks frightened and stands further away. Particles of dust fall away from the doors, which grate heavily as they open.* THE DOCTOR *peers into the gloom.*)

KLIEG: Come on.

THE DOCTOR: No. Wait, wait . . . I would be very careful in there, if I were you.

HAYDON: Well why wasn't Toberman killed? Why weren't you killed?

THE DOCTOR: The poor fellow who died drained all the electricity out of his body. It's perfectly safe to go in there now.

KLIEG: Come on then, we're wasting time.

(KLIEG *starts for the open door.* KAFTAN *takes* KLIEG'*s arm, and indicates* PARRY.)

Of course . . . after you, Professor.

(PARRY *leads the way, followed by* VINER, *excitedly polishing his glasses, and* HAYDON, KAFTAN, KLIEG *and* TOBERMAN.)

THE DOCTOR: But I'd . . . I'd still . . . I'd still be very careful if I were you. Very careful indeed.

(*He whispers to* VICTORIA).

Come on, let's go and join them.

(THE DOCTOR *and* JAMIE *move forward, but* VICTORIA *hangs back, looking frightened.* THE DOCTOR *turns to her.*)

Come on Victoria!

(*She doesn't move and* THE DOCTOR *walks up to her. In an attempt to overcome her fears, he deliberately changes the subject.*)

You look very nice in that dress, Victoria.

VICTORIA: Thank you. Don't you think it's a bit er . . .

THE DOCTOR: A bit short? Oh, I shouldn't worry about that – look at Jamie's!

JAMIE: Hey! I'll have you know . . .

(THE DOCTOR *winks at* JAMIE *who catches on.*)

. . . Oh, aye.

(VICTORIA *slowly breaks into a smile at this.*)

THE DOCTOR: Come along, come along. Let's go and see what the others are doing shall we? Come along.

(*As they enter,* JAMIE *and* THE DOCTOR *hold out their hands to* VICTORIA. *She stays behind, and the two men grasp each other's hands. As soon as they realise what they have done, they both release their hold, with some embar-rassment.*)

3. *TELOS CONTROL ROOM.*

(*On the right-hand side of the room is a bank of levers. Above them is a huge circular screen, divided into forty*

segments, each containing three sym-
bols. An arrow head, fixed to the
screen points upwards. On either side
of the screen, there are two similar,
but much smaller screens. One con-
tains a matrix of binary digits, and the
other, on the left-hand side, contains
roman numerals. Opposite this, on the
far side of the room is a small set of
open steps, leading to a sort of hatch,
which also has an arrow symbol
attached to it. The hatch is firmly
closed. Around the room are further
Cyberman motifs similar to the one on
the door of the tomb, although these
are of just the head of a Cyberman. In
the centre of the room is a circular
table, which has four stools around it.
On each stool, and on each corre-
sponding segment of the table there is
the same motif. There is dust every-
where and an air of decay. PARRY,
VINER *and* HAYDON *are inspecting the*
control panel.)

VICTORIA: Mercy! Just look at this place.

PARRY: These controls are of their earlier dynasties.

HAYDON: Not so very early, by the look of it. Look, John, it's . . .

VINER: Yes, I'm quite capable of making my own deductions, thank you.

HAYDON: All right.

(*The three men examine the control board and the symbol-filled screens.* KLIEG, KAFTAN *and* TOBERMAN *stand on the furthest side away from the control panel.*)

KLIEG: Be careful. There might be danger in there.

KAFTAN: Don't worry – with Toberman to guard me.

(*She lowers her voice and looks behind her.*)

What is more important is to keep an eye on these strangers.

KLIEG: I tried to get rid of them.

KAFTAN: Don't raise your voice, you will achieve nothing by shouting. You look after the Doctor and I will watch the girl.

KLIEG: And the Scots boy?

KAFTAN: Leave him to Toberman.

(*She smiles at* TOBERMAN.)

Eh, Toberman?

(TOBERMAN *smiles and clenches his huge hands as if round Jamie's neck.*)

But you will be careful and discreet. Understand?

TOBERMAN: I understand.

(*As the three of them join the others by the code machine,* THE DOCTOR, JAMIE *and* VICTORIA *enter.*)

JAMIE: Did ye ever see the like of it Doctor?

THE DOCTOR: Not exactly, Jamie, but very nearly.

(THE DOCTOR *starts examining the wall. He knocks slightly and listens, then examines it closely with a magnifying glass. He goes over and repeats his actions on the other side of the room.*)

PARRY: Now that we're all here . . .

(*He realises that not everyone is paying attention.*)

Ahem! Now that we're all here, I think we'd better take stock of the situation. This appears to be a dead end. The only way out appears to be through that hatch.

(*He goes over to the hatch.*)

KAFTAN: Are there no doors?

PARRY: No, apart from the entrance . . .

THE DOCTOR: And the other two, of course.

VINER: Two other doors?

(THE DOCTOR *points to a door immediately to the right of the control panel and, to another on the opposite side.*)

THE DOCTOR: Oh yes. One in that section, and one in that section over there. Activated, I imagine, by this simple logical system here. Here we are . . . er . . . I think.

(*He pulls one lever half way down, then two more all the way.*)

Yes, yes, a simple logical gate!

(*The door on the right side of the control slides away.* THE DOCTOR *performs the same sequence which opens the left-hand door.*)

KLIEG: Doctor, you seem to be very familiar with this place.

THE DOCTOR: Oh no, not really. It's all based on symbolic logic. The same as you use in computers. The opening mechanism for this door – an 'OR-gate', you call it.

KLIEG: Yes, yes I can see that, but how did you know in the first place?

(KLIEG *approaches* THE DOCTOR, *accusation in his eyes.*)

THE DOCTOR: Oh, I used my own special technique.

KLIEG: Oh really, Doctor . . . and may we know what that is?

THE DOCTOR: Keeping my eyes open and my mouth shut.

(HAYDON *laughs and even* KAFTAN *smiles.*)

PARRY: We are far too many to explore together. I think we'd better divide up. If you, Mr Viner, would take that door with . . . er . . .

(*He looks at* JAMIE.)

JAMIE: Jamie.

PARRY: Jamie and Mr. Haydon, Mr. Klieg, the Doctor and myself will make up the other party.

VICTORIA: What about us?

PARRY: I think the women had better remain here.

VICTORIA: Oh rubbish! We can make a party.

KAFTAN: Certainly. With Toberman to guard us, we need fear no one.

PARRY: Right. Mr. Klieg, would you take them along with you?

KLIEG: I'd prefer to stay here.

PARRY: As you wish. Mr. Viner, will you go along with the women?

VINER: If you like.

PARRY: But get back to the spacecraft by 16.30. You all know the temperature-drop at night, so we'll meet back here at 16.25. If anyone is missing, that will give us an hour to look for them before we have to leave.

(VINER *turns to the two women.*)

VINER: Come on then, we might as well try that opening over there.

(*He leads them off to the left.*)

KAFTAN: We'd better keep close together.

(*She offers her hand to* VICTORIA, *who is nervous of* KAFTAN. VICTORIA *smiles and shakes her head.*)

VICTORIA: I'm all right, thank you.

(*They leave with* VINER *and* TOBER-MAN.)

HAYDON: Come on, Jamie.

JAMIE: Right.

(*They exit.* PARRY *goes over to the hatch.*)

PARRY: Now to concentrate on this – whatever it is. This hatch must lead somewhere and there must be some opening mechanism. What was that about symbolic logic? Any ideas?

THE DOCTOR: No, not really. I think it's about time we gave Mr. Klieg a chance to show off his archaeological skills. I love to see the experts at work, don't you?

4. THE RECHARGING ROOM

(*Again the walls are metallic, with alternate matt and shiny stripes. On one side of the room is a huge, sarcophagus-like object. Its hinged lid is open and, inside, is the hollowed-out form of a Cyberman. From the top there emerge enormous cables leading to a machine covered in heavy studs, with two projector-like protuberances near its top, both trained on the sarcophagus.* VINER *enters, followed by* KAFTAN *and* VICTORIA.)

VINER: Come on – right in.

(*He looks around.*)

Where is Toberman?

KAFTAN: I sent him to join the others. We do not need any other protection now that you are with us.

(*She smiles at him and takes his arm.* VINER *moves back.*)

VINER: Yes . . . well, shall we commence?

(*He takes out a notebook and pencil.*)

Everything must be carefully measured and recorded.

VICTORIA: What is this room?

VINER: I don't know. Possibly, this is where the Cybermen are made.

> (VICTORIA *goes over to the machine and touches it.*)

VICTORIA: I wonder what this is?

VINER: Do you mind? You're getting in my way. Just go over there, will you?

> (*He waves a hand towards the centre of the room.* VICTORIA *obeys and goes over to the sarcophagus.*)

VICTORIA: Oh, fiddle!

> (KAFTAN *has moved over to the wall and is inspecting the machinery.*)

KAFTAN: Could this not be the purpose of the room?

VINER: Yes?

KAFTAN: A Cyberman would stand in that form and be, well . . . revitalised.

VINER: Yes. That's reasonable.

> (*He points to the projector-like apparatus.*)

These projectors were probably made to fire in some sort of neuro-electric potential. Yes that's it, I think you're right.

(VICTORIA *is now standing in the empty form of the Cyberman.*)

VICTORIA: Revitalising is just what I need. Oh mercy! The Cybermen must have been giants!

(VINER *sees what* VICTORIA *is doing and quickly goes over to her.*)

VINER: Will you please be careful? The first rule of archaeological work is that *nothing* must be touched until it has been described and recorded!

(*He turns away and* VICTORIA *pulls a face at his back. She runs her hand round the inside of the sarcophagus.* KAFTAN *looks around furtively, making sure that no one is watching her. She finds what looks like the power switch, and looking over at* VICTORIA, *presses it down.* KAFTAN *waits expectantly, but nothing happens. She registers angry disappointment.*)

5. *THE TESTING ROOM.*

(*At one end of the room are a pair of tightly closed doors.*)

JAMIE: You know – it's just struck me. All the corridors in here are as light as day, yet there are no windows!

HAYDON: Alpha-meson phosphor.

JAMIE: Eh?

HAYDON: It's a lighting system that never goes out. Works by letting cosmic rays bombard a layer of barium on a . . .

JAMIE: Oh aye that, yeah.

HAYDON: Point is . . . what is this room used for?

JAMIE (*oov*): Possibly for raising caterpillars.

HAYDON: Eh?

JAMIE: Like this one.

>   (*He rises into view holding a Cybermat in his hand. It is metallic, silver, and about a foot long, with a segmented tail. It has two eyes and a pair of antennae. It appears to be totally inert.*)

HAYDON: For heaven's sake watch out, until we know what it is!

JAMIE: Och, it's as dead as a stone.

6. THE CONTROL ROOM.

>   (KLIEG *is operating some of the levers below the code machine.* PARRY *is watching over his shoulder.* THE DOCTOR *is over by the hatch, examining it.* TOBERMAN *enters and stealthily slips past to the exterior doors, unnoticed.*)

PARRY: Well?

> (KLIEG *points to the two small screens, either side of the central display.*)

KLIEG: Well, the basis of this code is binary to digital conversion with an intervening step involving a sort of a Whitehead logic. When this Fourier series is complete, then there is no more to be done.

> (*He points again to the Roman numerals.*)

THE DOCTOR: Yes, but why do it at all?

PARRY: Really Doctor, for an archaeologist you seem to be curiously lacking in curiosity.

THE DOCTOR: Some things are better left undone – and I have a feeling that this is one of them.

KLIEG: What do you mean by that?

THE DOCTOR: Well, it's all too easy, isn't it?

KLIEG: Easy!

PARRY: I wouldn't call this an easy survey, would you, Klieg?

KLIEG: Everything here is designed to keep their secrets, whatever they are, insoluble.

THE DOCTOR: Insoluble? Oh, I wouldn't say that.

KLIEG: But take this mathematical sequence for example. I'm really no nearer to its solution. I've tried every possible combination. You'd hardly call that easy.

(THE DOCTOR *takes* KLIEG's *notepad.*)

THE DOCTOR: Yes, well . . . what you have done here is mostly right.

(KLIEG *sarcastically replies.*)

KLIEG: Oh, thank you!

THE DOCTOR: You see, if you take any progressive series, it can be converted into binary notation. If you take the sum of the integrants and express the result as a power series, then the indices show the basic binary blocks.

(KLIEG *starts forward.* THE DOCTOR *restrains him.*)

Only I wouldn't do it if I were you. Oh no, I really wouldn't do it!

(KLIEG *snatches back his pad from* THE DOCTOR, *and starts to read off the combination of figures onto the dial.*)

KLIEG: Of course, you're right! Look, sum between limits of 1 and 91 integral into power series, yes, yes . . . Then you differentiate . . .

(*The machine comes to life. The pointer is moving by itself.* KLIEG *backs away in horror.*)

THE DOCTOR: You fool! Why couldn't you leave it alone?

> (*There is a loud rumbling from below them. The room shakes as in an earthquake. The main lights flicker on and off. The control panel lights up. The table is illuminated from within. A muffled pounding starts from below the room.*)

PARRY: What's happening?

THE DOCTOR: I don't know. Perhaps the Cybermen aren't quite as dormant as you imagine. We must find out what's happened to the others!

> (*He hurries out.*)

7. THE RECHARGING ROOM.

> (*The rumbling and throbbing is heard here, only a little fainter than in the Control Room. VINER looks round for the source of the noise. Behind KAFTAN, the control board lights come on. She reacts fearfully but now sees her chance. Screwing up her courage, she grasps the power lever and pulls it down. As she does so, the lid of the sarcophagus begins to close on VICTORIA. She tries to get out, but is unable to do so. She screams. The door closes completely. VINER turns angrily to KAFTAN.*)

VINER: Did you touch anything?

KAFTAN: No.

VINER: Well, keep away from that board.

            (*He rushes to the sarcophagus, and tries desperately to pull it open.*)

            Here – help me!

KAFTAN: One moment.

            (KAFTAN *looks at the control board, and moves her hand towards the power lever.*)

VINER: Now!

            (KAFTAN *pulls her hand away and runs over to* VINER. *They both tug at the closed form.*)

            We'll need a crowbar to get this off!

KAFTAN: It may already be too late.

            8. *THE TESTING ROOM.*

            (JAMIE *is still looking at the Cybermat on the ground.*)

JAMIE: That's strange.

HAYDON: What?

JAMIE: I could swear that thing moved.

HAYDON: You're seeing things, old chap. Come and look at this. The whole control panel is active, suddenly. Don't know which button to press first.

JAMIE: I wouldn't touch it if I were you.

(HAYDON *ignores* JAMIE.)

HAYDON: I think I'll try this one.

(*He pushes a button and looks expectantly round the room.*)

Nothing.

(*The lights start to dim.*)

JAMIE: Wait a moment. What's happening? It's getting dark. Hey, look at the far wall.

(HAYDON *follows* JAMIE's *gaze. On the wall at the far end we see a shape beginning to form. A series of circles appears.* JAMIE *stares as if hypnotised.*)

9. THE RECHARGING ROOM.

(VINER *is studying the control board.*)

VINER: It's no use, I daren't touch anything. If I operate the wrong sequence she'll die. I must find the logical order. ·

(*He turns and looks at* KAFTAN *by the sarcophagus.*)

If it's not too late.

(KAFTAN *motions him to listen. She raps several times on the cover. There are answering raps.* VINER *comes over to join* KAFTAN.)

KAFTAN: She is still alive.

VINER: Thank heavens! Look I'd better go and get the others. You stay here with her, will you?

KAFTAN: Yes . . . well, hurry!

VINER: I won't be long.

(KAFTAN, *left alone, smiles to herself. She taps again on the casing. Again there are several answering knocks.* KAFTAN *goes to the control panel and grasps two levers, one in each hand. As she moves them up and down, left and right, the 'nozzles' of the projectors move in unison. They begin to pulsate. A powerful, low, pulsing buzz fills the room.* THE DOCTOR *enters with* VINER *and takes in the situation at a glance.* KAFTAN *is startled and turns away from the control board in frustration. Concealed by her body, she furtively tries to move her hands back to the controls.*)

THE DOCTOR: I wouldn't touch the projector controls, if I were you.

(*He steps up beside her.*)

Someone might get hurt.

(VINER *joins them at the control board.*)

VINER: There must be some way to release it, Doctor.

THE DOCTOR: Yes there is – now let me see . . .

(*He studies the panel and various levers.*)

10. *THE TESTING ROOM.*

(JAMIE *and* HAYDON *are staring, hypnotised, at the moving circles.* HAYDON *with a great effort breaks the spell and reels back.* JAMIE *remains transfixed.*)

HAYDON: Jamie. Jamie!

(*He holds his hands in front of his face to shield his eyes from the hypnotic shapes.*)

Don't watch it!

JAMIE: I must, I must. I can't seem to take my eyes off it – I don't want to take my eyes off it . . . I don't want to take my . . .

HAYDON: Stop, Jamie!

(JAMIE *is slowly moving towards the pulsating wall. The shapes seem to expand as he moves towards them.* HAYDON *grasps his arm but* JAMIE *pulls it away.*)

JAMIE: Yes, yes, I see it now.

(*He continues to move slowly towards the wall. In desperation,* HAYDON *goes back to the panel and presses a button, then another. The shapes change. Finally when* JAMIE *is right in front of the wall, he presses another button, and the shapes fade.* JAMIE *stands transfixed for a moment and then turns back.*)

HAYDON: Are you all right?

JAMIE: Where have I been?

(*He raises his hands to his head.* HAYDON *watches anxiously.*)

HAYDON: You've been under some form of hypnosis.

JAMIE: That's ridiculous. What would the Cybermen want with a hypnotising machine?

HAYDON: Yes, you're right – must be for something else. Wait a minute, know what it could be?

JAMIE: What?

HAYDON: Some kind of target – I remember reading about this somewhere. They used to have something like it on Earth years ago.

JAMIE: How does it work – which bit do you aim at?

HAYDON: There is a subliminal centre which you are trained to see.

JAMIE: Oh aye – a what?

HAYDON: Come on, let's run the whole thing again and see what happens, but keep your eyes off the wall – now you work the controls this time and I'll watch.

JAMIE: Right.

(*He crosses to the controls.*)

HAYDON: O.K., press the buttons!

11. *The Recharging Room.*

(THE DOCTOR *has found what he believes to be the releasing switch.*)

THE DOCTOR: Yes, I think this is the sequence. Stand by to let her out will you?

(VINER *nods.* KAFTAN *stands by watching intently.*)

And if you, my dear, would stand well clear? Thank you.

(KAFTAN *looks at him. He gives her a charming smile that does not minimise the implication of his words. She moves back.*)

Right.

(*He pulls some levers in a particular order. The sarcophagus swings open.* THE DOCTOR *hurries over.* VINER *helps her out.*)

Victoria! Are you all right?

(*She clings to* THE DOCTOR, *sobbing.*)

It's all right. Get your breath. It's all right. It's all right now.

VICTORIA: I didn't like that very much, Doctor.

THE DOCTOR: It's all right. I don't expect you did. You'll have to be a little more careful in future, won't you?

(THE DOCTOR *looks over his shoulder at* KAFTAN *as he speaks – she turns away.*)

Now come along, we must go and see whether Jamie is all right. Come along!

(*They turn towards the door, followed by* VINER *and* KAFTAN.)

12. THE CONTROL ROOM.

PARRY: There must be some way to get that hatch open.

KLIEG: That must be the control to do it.

(*He indicates a lever and operates it. It doesn't work.*)

PARRY: The tombs of the Cybermen must be below ground, together with all their records. If we can't get down there all our work here, and the sacrifice of that unfortunate fellow's life, will go in vain.

(KLIEG *murmurs to himself.*)

KLIEG: A great deal more than that . . .

PARRY: Pardon?

KLIEG: Of course, there's only one explanation. The Doctor!

PARRY: Yes?

KLIEG: He didn't give us the complete code. There must be a further sequence to operate that opening mechanism.

PARRY: All right. Well let's try and find out.

KLIEG: Now – what could it be?

(*He starts trying to work it out from the figures already on the wall.*)

13. THE TESTING ROOM.

(*The shapes are moving across the wall.* JAMIE *is working the controls,* HAYDON *is shielding his eyes with his hands.*)

HAYDON: Is that all?

JAMIE: Aye – all except this big button here. What does that do?

HAYDON: I'm not sure – but we'll soon find out.

(*He goes to the far wall.*)

I'm going to trace the source of these shapes. There must be a projector somewhere. Look, when I give the word, press the button.

JAMIE: The big one?

HAYDON: Yes, maybe it works in conjunction with the others.

JAMIE: Right, ready when you are.

HAYDON: O.K. go ahead!

(JAMIE *starts to press the button. The far end of the room lights up, and there is a whirring sound. The doors at the far end of the room start to open.* THE DOCTOR, *followed by* VICTORIA *and* VINER, *enters from another way.* HAYDON *remains in front of the wall.*)

THE DOCTOR: Jamie! Don't touch that control!

JAMIE: I already have. What's the matter, Doctor?

(THE DOCTOR *rushes over to the controls and tries to revert the controls that* JAMIE *has operated. He is working with desperate speed.*)

THE DOCTOR: Which one was it?

JAMIE: Which one what?

(*The doors are now almost fully open. We hear something approaching. Then out of the blackness looms a silver figure. A Cyberman appears and raises his gun. There is a flash.* HAYDON *twitches, smoke pouring from him. The others huddle together.* VICTORIA *screams.*)

1. *THE TESTING ROOM.*

THE DOCTOR: Jamie! Don't touch that control!

JAMIE: I already have. What's the matter Doctor?

(THE DOCTOR *rushes over to the console, and tries to revert the controls that* JAMIE *has operated. He is working with desperate speed.*)

THE DOCTOR: Which one was it?

JAMIE: Which one what?

(*The doors are now almost fully open. We hear something approaching. Then out of the blackness looms a silver figure. A Cyberman appears and raises his gun. There is a flash.* HAYDON *twitches, smoke pouring from him. The others huddle together. The doors close on the Cyberman again.* VICTORIA *makes a move towards* HAYDON. THE DOCTOR *stops her. There is a sound of machinery running down. The noise stops.* VINER *and* THE DOCTOR *examine the body.* THE DOCTOR *straightens up and turns to* JAMIE.)

THE DOCTOR: What exactly happened here, Jamie? What did you do? What sequence did you use?

JAMIE: Sequence? How do you mean . . . Oh, you mean these. Well, I just pressed that button . . . and pulled this lever . . . and then . . .

(PARRY *enters.*)

PARRY: Doctor – if you could spare us a moment, I . . .

(*He suddenly sees* HAYDON's *body.*)

Haydon! What's happened?

(VINER *reacts hysterically.*)

VINER: He's dead, don't you see, he's dead! It's this damned building. It's alive, it's watching us, it'll get us all. We've got to leave!

PARRY: All right, Viner. This is terrible! How did it happen?

VINER: We've got to get out of this building! It's deadly! They'll kill all of us if we don't get back to the rocket!

THE DOCTOR: They?

VINER: The Cybermen! Didn't you see it?

(THE DOCTOR *examines the doors.*)

PARRY: A Cyberman. A *live* Cyberman! My dear
Viner, they've been dead for the last five
hundred years.

VINER: I tell you it was a Cyberman and it came out
of there! That . . . that screen thing.

JAMIE: He's right.

(PARRY *moves towards the screen.*)

VINER: Keep back, keep back! You'll bring it out
again.

THE DOCTOR: The question is, what killed him?

VICTORIA: But you saw the Cyberman, Doctor!

THE DOCTOR: I saw something.

VINER: Well?

THE DOCTOR: Poor Haydon was looking at that screen. In
the direction we all were – right?

VINER: Of course. Must you state the obvious?

THE DOCTOR: It's not so obvious when you consider . . .
he was shot in the back.

JAMIE: In the back?

PARRY: Are you sure, Doctor?

THE DOCTOR: See for yourself.

(PARRY *and* VINER *come over to examine Haydon's body.* THE DOCTOR *looks round the room.*)

Now, if the Cyberman didn't shoot him, what did? The answer, I think, lies over here. Jamie . . .

(*He goes over to the rear wall.*)

JAMIE:	Yes Doctor?
THE DOCTOR:	Can you remember exactly what you did? What sequence you used?
JAMIE:	Oh! I'm not sure, Doctor.
THE DOCTOR:	You must try. I want you to repeat it all when I give you the word.
JAMIE:	Very well, Doctor.
VINER:	You're crazy, man! You'll bring that . . . that . . . thing out again.
THE DOCTOR:	Maybe. I don't know. Now Jamie, when you're ready.
JAMIE:	Anytime, Doctor.
THE DOCTOR:	Now, there is a distinct element of risk in what I'm asking you all to do, so if anyone wishes to leave, they must do so at once.

(JAMIE *starts to leave.*)

Not you Jamie.

VINER:	Can't you stop this? He'll kill us all.

THE DOCTOR: Not if you go back against the wall. In the corner there . . . now please.

> (VINER *goes and joins the others by the wall.*)

Right, Jamie.

> (JAMIE *presses the buttons, and again the lights flash and the doors open. A panel at the far end is seen to slide back and a gun-like object fires at the Cyberman as he appears in the open doors. The Cyberman's head blows off.* VICTORIA *screams again.* THE DOCTOR *leans across the controls and throws a switch. Both the doors and the panel remain open.* THE DOCTOR *cautiously moves forward.*)

JAMIE: Careful Doctor . . .

THE DOCTOR: It's all right . . . I think. I think it's all right now.

> (*The Cyberman is composed of a steel skeleton, full of complex mechanical apparatus. One arm is outstretched, and is holding a weapon.*)

Yes, you see it's just a mock-up . . . a model.

> (PARRY *goes to touch the gun.*)

No, no don't touch that . . . that gun may be wired up too!

VINER: It's a trap!

THE DOCTOR: No I don't think so. I think it's a testing room for weapons. This is a purely robotic Cyberman. There's no human material in it at all. He's a target . . . for weapons.

PARRY: Let's get back to the control room with this poor fellow.

(VINER *and* JAMIE *pick up* HAYDON'S *body and they turn to leave. As they do,* VICTORIA *spots the Cybermat, still on the ground.*)

VICTORIA: What's that?

JAMIE: Some wee creature I found on the floor there.

VICTORIA: It's a fossil.

THE DOCTOR: Victoria! Be careful. Let me see that.

(*He approaches* VICTORIA.)

Yes, it's certainly inactive. But it's not a fossil. Wait a minute.

(*He fishes his five-hundred-year diary out of his pocket, and searches through it.*)

Yes, here we are – yes, it's a *Cybermat*!

VICTORIA: What's a Cybermat?

THE DOCTOR: It's one of those . . . I'd leave it alone if I were you. Come along.

> (*He exits*. VICTORIA *makes a face at his back and she places the Cybermat in her handbag*.)

2. THE CONTROL ROOM (INTERIOR).

> (KAFTAN *is standing by* KLIEG, *who is still working on the code*. TOBERMAN *enters from the main entrance to the tomb*. KAFTAN *looks at him*.)

KAFTAN: Well?

TOBERMAN: It is done.

KAFTAN: Good.

KLIEG: I just don't understand this code. This sequence doesn't make complete sense.

KAFTAN: You a logician, you can't understand it? You must!

KLIEG: In the time . . . In the time we have . . .

KAFTAN: We have plenty of time – you will see.

(KLIEG *shrugs and turns back to his work.* PARRY *enters, followed by* JAMIE *and* VINER *carrying the body, which they place out of sight behind the table and cover with* VINER's *coat.* THE DOCTOR *enters followed by* VICTORIA. *She puts her bag down by the table.*)

PARRY: Lay him down there.

KAFTAN: What has happened to him?

VINER: There has been a terrible accident. He has been shot.

PARRY: Right, we're all here, it seems. Will you all sit down for a moment?

KAFTAN: Toberman.

TOBERMAN: Yes.

(*They all sit round the table, except* KLIEG, *who carries on working.*)

PARRY: Mr. Klieg?

KLIEG: Leave me alone, will you? Can't you see I'm working? Or have you forgotten the purpose of this expedition?

PARRY: This directly concerns *my* expedition. You will kindly take your place.

(KLIEG *comes over, with obvious bad grace, and sits at the table.*)

Right, I'll come straight to the point. I have reluctantly decided to abandon the expedition and return to Earth.

(*There is a storm of protest.* PARRY *raises his hands for silence.*)

I feel as strongly about it as you – this expedition has been my dream for many years. But there were those, like Mr. Viner, who said that more preparation was needed. More men and equipment. I refused to heed their warnings and the result is that two men have died. I'm sorry, but we must leave at the first available conjunction. We'll take back all we can for further study of course – but that is my decision, and that is what we must do.

KLIEG: I insist that . . .

(KAFTAN *stops him with a reassuring touch of the hand.* THE DOCTOR *notices this.*)

PARRY: My decision is final. We leave when the north hemisphere is properly tangential, which will be at . . .

(*He consults his Unit Chronometer.*)

. . . 18.42.

(*They all start to rise. As they do,* HOPPER *bursts in, out of breath.*)

Ah, Captain Hopper, just the man. Can you be ready to blast off at 18.42?

(HOPPER *tries hard to catch his breath.*)

HOPPER: No!

PARRY: I beg your pardon. Did I hear you right? You are paid to take orders, Captain Hopper.

HOPPER: Not impossible ones, I'm not. It's the fuel pumps. Some character has balled-up the lot!

(*There is a chorus of disbelief.*)

THE DOCTOR: Or some . . . thing?

HOPPER: Well, whatever it is, it's practically wrecked our chances of getting off this crumby planet.

(*They all react. The unchanging faces of the Cyberman motifs stare down at them from the wall.*)

3. *THE CONTROL ROOM* (*EVENING*).

VINER: I don't care what any of you say, I utterly refuse! I will not spend the night on this planet.

THE DOCTOR: I don't think we've got much choice.

VINER: Well, at least we can get out of this sinister building.

(*He looks round nervously and taps his notebook.*)

I have recorded all the necessary details. I suggest we all go back to the rocket.

(HOPPER *enters in time to hear this.*)

HOPPER: That's a very bad suggestion Viner, you know that.

VINER: I insist.

HOPPER: You do a lot of insisting. Well I'm going to tell you something now. The first guy that steps into my rocket-ship is going to stop the repair work just like that.

(*He snaps his fingers.*)

PARRY: How long will it take to get the rocket operational again?

HOPPER: Working non-stop . . . without interruption? Maybe . . . seventy-two hours.

(*They all react to this.*)

VINER: Well, that's impossible, we'd all be out of our minds after three days in this place. We must go back on board.

HOPPER: Look, I can't afford to waste any more time with you guys, but I'll give it to you once more, all right? Now, you may not know this but we have to practically pull that ship apart to fix the damage, and there just isn't room for all of you on board.

(*He looks at* VINER.)

Especially with you insisting all over the place. NO . . . ROOM . . . TO . . . WORK. Got it?

PARRY: Yes of course, I see now . . .

VINER: It's all right for you – have you any idea of what it's like in this deadly building?

HOPPER: Well, it's not exactly peaches back on the ship.

THE DOCTOR: Captain you . . . you do have another reason for not wanting them back on the ship, don't you?

HOPPER: Yeah – until I find out who broke into that rocket . . .

THE DOCTOR: Or what . . .

HOPPER: *Who* broke into the rocket! Until then I'm going to keep a round-the-clock guard on it.

THE DOCTOR: I see.

HOPPER: I'm going to get off this place with my skin still fitting tight all over – all right?

THE DOCTOR: All right.

HOPPER: Now in case it gets cold at night, I've brought these anoraks and some food. I'll let you know when I'm ready to take off.

(HOPPER *exits.*)

KLIEG: As we have to stay, we might as well finish our job and fully explore down there.

(*He jerks his thumb downwards.*)

That is . . . if the Professor has no objection?

PARRY: We have no alternative, it seems.

THE DOCTOR: Well, but . . . can't we stay here?

(*He looks round.*)

. . . It seems a pleasant enough room to me.

JAMIE: Hey! You speak for yourself.

KLIEG: Of course, you can leave here any time you please, Doctor.

(*He goes over to the control board and resumes work on the code.*)

THE DOCTOR: Oh yes . . . I was forgetting. I can, can't I?

VICTORIA: But you're not going to, are you Doctor?

THE DOCTOR: No, not just yet awhile – no.

(KAFTAN *goes over to join* KLIEG *at the control board.*)

But you and Jamie can go back to the
TARDIS if you wish.

VICTORIA: I'll stay with you.

THE DOCTOR: Jamie?

JAMIE: Oh, I'll stay.

THE DOCTOR: Good.

(*He suddenly steps into action, going
over to* KLIEG *and* KAFTAN.)

Well now, I think it's about time we gave
Mr. Klieg some help.

KLIEG: Thank you, I think I can manage.

(TOBERMAN *blocks* THE DOCTOR's
way.)

TOBERMAN: Stay!

JAMIE: Hey! Let the Doctor pass, or I'll . . . yes,
well, let the Doctor pass.

THE DOCTOR: It's all right, Jamie.

(*He looks at* KAFTAN.)

Your colleague has . . . very strong hands.

KAFTAN: Very strong.

THE DOCTOR: Enough to do a good deal of damage – if let
loose in the right place.

(KAFTAN *stares at* THE DOCTOR *for a moment, then nods to* TOBERMAN. *He moves aside.* THE DOCTOR *stands beside* KLIEG *at the control panel and studies his figures.* VICTORIA *shivers and moves closer to* JAMIE. PARRY *and* VINER *remain at the table studying a plan* VINER *is drawing of the layout of* TELOS.)

PARRY: There's no doubt about it. The major workings lie below. There are metal caverns down there all interconnected. If only we can get down into them.

KLIEG: That's it. I've done it. Finally, a Boolean function of symbolic logic!

THE DOCTOR: Logical yes, but . . .

KAFTAN: Everything yields to logic – our basic assumption, Doctor.

THE DOCTOR: Really?

(KLIEG *is feverishly working the indicator and handle.*)

KLIEG: 6 cap B4 if, and only if, C is cap function of 2A.

(*He presses a lever and stands back. Nothing happens.*)

THE DOCTOR: I think perhaps your logic is wearing a little thin.

KLIEG: I must have made a mistake. I'll do it again, more carefully.

THE DOCTOR: Yes.

KLIEG: 6 cap B4 if, and only if, C is cap function of Ah . . . that's it . . . 2F not 2A!

(*Whilst he does this,* THE DOCTOR, *unseen by the rest, quietly flicks a switch. The hatch slowly begins to open.*)

VICTORIA: The hatch. Look!

KLIEG: I've done it. I've done it!

THE DOCTOR: Congratulations.

JAMIE: But Doctor . . .

(THE DOCTOR *puts his finger to his lips, to silence* JAMIE.)

PARRY: Excellent. Now – to work. It will be extremely cold down there. We shall all need to put on warm clothing. Mr. Viner, will you please see about the anoraks?

(VINER *does so.*)

KLIEG: But, just a moment. Are we all going down?

PARRY: There is safety in numbers.

KLIEG: The women as well?

PARRY: They, of course, will stay up here.

(*He turns to* KAFTAN *and* VICTORIA.)

In case of trouble, contact the rocket.

(*He goes over to put on a warm anorak. The others do the same.*)

VICTORIA: I'm coming down with you.

PARRY: But my dear young lady . . .

VICTORIA: You heard me, Professor.

THE DOCTOR: Victoria . . .

(*He draws her aside.*)

You would be much safer up here.

VICTORIA: But Doctor I . . .

(THE DOCTOR *lowers his voice to a whisper.*)

THE DOCTOR: . . . and much more use to us.

VICTORIA: I don't see . . .

THE DOCTOR: Keep an eye on things . . . please.

VICTORIA: All right.

THE DOCTOR: Thank you.

PARRY: Well, if we are all ready, I shall lead the descent. Be ready to go back the instant I give the word.

(KLIEG *is about to enter but steps aside to speak to* KAFTAN.)

KLIEG: You know what to do?

KAFTAN: The hatch?

(KLIEG *nods. Over at the open hatch,* PARRY *is lowering himself down, followed by* VINER *and* JAMIE.)

THE DOCTOR: Toberman?

KAFTAN: He stays with me.

THE DOCTOR: Then I stay here too.

(*He smiles, folds his arms, and sits down on one of the stools.*)

KAFTAN: Of course, I am being selfish. His strength will be useful to you down there. He must go down . . . Go down Toberman.

(TOBERMAN *nods, eyeing* THE DOCTOR *suspiciously, and goes down.* THE DOCTOR *whispers to* VICTORIA.)

THE DOCTOR: . . . what I said: be very careful!

(*He follows* TOBERMAN *down.*)

KAFTAN: It seems we are to be left alone – to wait.

(VICTORIA *nods nervously, and clutches her bag.*)

Captain Hopper brought some food from the rocket. You would like some?

VICTORIA: Oh, rather! I'm ravenous.

(*The Cybermat moves slightly, unnoticed by* VICTORIA. KAFTAN *goes to an aluminium mesh rectangular box. Inside are some transparent plastic containers.*)

KAFTAN: Roast beef? Roast veal? Chicken?

VICTORIA: Oh, chicken please.

(KAFTAN *passes her a rectangular plastic covered lump.*)

What on Earth's this?

KAFTAN: What you have asked for – chicken.

(VICTORIA *looks at it, sniffs it distastefully and passes it back to* KAFTAN.)

VICTORIA: Thank you, but er . . . I'm not very hungry now.

4. *A PASSAGE WITHIN THE CYBER TOMB.*

(*The group of explorers is in a tunnel made of bright metal. There is a massive ladder leading down from the hatch in the control room above. There is a covering of frost and ice. Their feet crunch underfoot.* TOBERMAN *and* THE DOCTOR *climb down the ladder to join them.*)

PARRY: Hurry up there, we've no time to linger. It's extremely cold down here, even with these anoraks.

(JAMIE *looks suspiciously at* KLIEG.)

JAMIE: Aye, you obviously knew what to expect.

THE DOCTOR: Well, which way do we go?

KLIEG: I don't know. Let's try this one.

VINER: Yes.

(KLIEG *flashes a torch along the passage ahead and leads off.*)

5. *THE CYBER TOMB.*

(*The group leaves the exit of the tunnel, and moves slowly into the tomb cavern. We see a huge array of frost-covered cells, reaching far up into the gloom.*)

JAMIE: Hey! What on Earth . . .

PARRY: Behold Gentlemen, the tombs of the Cybermen.

JAMIE: Tombs? I don't see any tombs.

THE DOCTOR: In there Jamie, frozen forever. All their evil locked away with them.

(*He murmurs to himself.*)

And so it must remain.

KLIEG: Like a gigantic honeycomb. Like bees waiting for the signal to arise from their winter sleep.

THE DOCTOR: A signal that they are never going to get.

(KLIEG *smiles and turns away to study a nearby control console.*)

VINER: We'd better get busy. Everything must be recorded. It is too cold to remain for long.

(*He takes notes as he speaks.*)

KLIEG: Unless we find some way to warm things up.

(THE DOCTOR *looks at him with growing suspicion.*)

6. *THE CONTROL ROOM.*

(VICTORIA *is sitting against the table trying to keep awake.* KAFTAN *is watching her intently.*)

KAFTAN: You have hardly touched your coffee. It must be cold by now. You would like some more?

(VICTORIA *replies drowsily.*)

VICTORIA: Thank you. I'm much warmer now.

KAFTAN: That's good.

VICTORIA: I . . . feel so sleepy.

> (*Her head settles back against the table. She drops off to sleep.* KAFTAN *tiptoes over to look at her. Satisfied that* VICTORIA *is asleep she crosses to the control board and operates the hatch opening control sequence. There is a grinding of gears and the hatch lid slowly starts to swing shut. It closes with a final clang.*)

7. *THE CYBER TOMB.*

> (*The sound echoes through the passageway. The men start.*)

VINER: What was that?

JAMIE: It sounded like the hatch.

> (*Only* KLIEG *and* TOBERMAN *fail to react to the noise, but they exchange glances.* JAMIE *rushes out followed by* VINER. KLIEG *turns back to the control panel.*)

8. *A PASSAGE WITHIN THE CYBER TOMB.*

> (JAMIE *and* VINER *run to the foot of the ladder and look up.*)

JAMIE: It's closed!

(JAMIE *climbs up the ladder.* VINER *starts to follow then climbs back down.*)

VINER: Oh what's the use? We're trapped down here now. We'll never survive in this cold. Better get back.

(VINER *makes his way back down the passage.*)

9. *THE CYBER TOMB.*

(THE DOCTOR *goes to meet* VINER.)

THE DOCTOR: Well?

VINER: It's closed. What have they done that for? What are they playing at up there?

THE DOCTOR: Perhaps it wasn't them. Where's Jamie?

VINER: He went up the ladder to try it.

(VINER *goes over to* PARRY.)

VINER: Professor.

(PARRY *waves him to silence, and takes another photograph.* VINER's *nerves start to crack.*)

Professor, listen to me, for heaven's sake. The hatch is down again. We're trapped down here.

KLIEG: Trapped?

PARRY: But there are some of my party up there. Are you sure?

VINER: Of course I'm sure. You know how heavy that thing is. It's down now. We must do something. I'd give us a couple of hours in here at the most.

THE DOCTOR: Mr. Klieg doesn't seem to be very worried.

KLIEG: No I'm not, Doctor.

(JAMIE *returns.*)

JAMIE: It won't open, and I can't make anybody hear.

VINER: There you are!

KLIEG: There is an easy way out of our situation.

VINER: You've found something?

KLIEG: Of course, you're forgetting your logic. If it closes it can be opened – from here.

(*He points to the control console.* THE DOCTOR *goes over and examines it.*)

THE DOCTOR: Conveniently labelled in symbolic logic, I notice.

KLIEG: Right, are we ready? I shall now operate the sequence.

THE DOCTOR: If it *is* the opening device.

(KLIEG *smiles at* THE DOCTOR.)

KLIEG: It is obviously an opening device of some kind, Doctor.

VINER: I don't know how you can be so blasted calm about it all!

(JAMIE *goes over to the passage.*)

JAMIE: I'll see if it works then. Go ahead.

(KLIEG *operates a series of controls, each labelled with Boolean and symbolic logic symbols.*)

JAMIE (*oov*): Nothing's happening out here.

VINER: It doesn't work.

(*The men are looking down the passage, and so fail to notice what is happening behind them. Except for* KLIEG *who turns round and smiles at what he sees. A drop of water falls on* PARRY's *cheek.*)

PARRY: Water!

JAMIE: Aye it's getting warmer.

VINER: The ice is melting.

JAMIE: Hey, look. Behind you!

(*They see the tomb beginning to melt.*

Water runs down the front of the cells, in ever increasing amounts.)

VINER: Look . . . look at the honeycomb. There's something inside!

JAMIE: They're . . . Cybermen!

(KLIEG moves back towards the control console, his face triumphant.)

THE DOCTOR: Jamie. Come back!

(The rate of de-freezing is accelerating. The figures of the Cybermen become clearer inside the cells.)

PARRY: It is them!

(He talks in an almost reverential whisper.)

Gentlemen they are perfect. This is unique in archaeology.

VINER: No . . . No . . . They're moving . . .

(KLIEG passes VINER as he slowly approaches the tombs. VINER backs away.)

VINER: We must shut it down.

(He rushes to the control console and

operates the last of the controls in reverse. At once frost begins to form again on the cells and the lights which had grown brighter begin to fade.)

KLIEG: What are you doing? Keep away from that.

VINER: No!

(PARRY _and_ JAMIE _step towards_ KLIEG. TOBERMAN _steps in front of him._)

PARRY: What are you doing, man?

(KLIEG _draws a gun._)

KLIEG: Keep back! I shall not hesitate to kill. For the last time, I am asking you to keep away from those controls.

VINER: No!

(_A shot rings out._ VINER _clutches his chest. He slumps, wounded, by the controls._)

PARRY: Viner! Viner, Viner, Viner . . . You've killed him!

JAMIE: He's mad.

THE DOCTOR: Jamie!

(KLIEG _springs forward and pulls the lever down again. The lights behind_

*the cells brighten again and, inside
them, the Cybermen again come to
life. Slowly they begin to break out
from their cells.)*

PARRY: Haydon dead, now Viner. What kind of
man are you?

KLIEG: Back . . . keep back. Let's see what
happens. As the Professor says – this is a
unique archaeological event. It would be
such a pity to miss it.

10. THE CONTROL ROOM.

*(KAFTAN is over by the controls mak-
ing notes on the logical sequence of the
opening controls. VICTORIA is still asleep by the table. She stirs, and we see
her hand is against the bag with the
Cybermat inside. VICTORIA pulls her
hand away. She wakes up, looks
around and sees KAFTAN by the controls. She rubs the sleep from her
eyes.)*

VICTORIA: What's happened?

KAFTAN: What?

VICTORIA: The hatch is down. Are they back?

KAFTAN: They are still down there.

VICTORIA: Then why is the hatch down? They won't be
able to get up again.

KAFTAN: I shall open it when we are ready.

VICTORIA: When who's ready? You closed it.

KAFTAN: I did.

VICTORIA: Then you'd better open it again, hadn't
             you?

KAFTAN: No, it shall remain closed.

             (VICTORIA _furiously turns on_ KAFTAN.)

VICTORIA: The Doctor warned me about you!

KAFTAN: That was very clever of him.

VICTORIA: Out of my way.

KAFTAN: Why?

VICTORIA: I'm going to open the hatch.

             (_She pushes_ KAFTAN _out of the way,
             and looks desperately at the controls._
             KAFTAN _pulls a small futuristic hand
             gun out of a pocket, and places it
             against_ VICTORIA_'s back._)

KAFTAN: Stand back.

             (VICTORIA _turns slowly round to face
             her._)

             That's better. Now let's move away from
             those controls. We shall be more
             comfortable over here, I think.

             (_The two women move back to the_

table. KAFTAN *keeping* VICTORIA *covered by the gun.* KAFTAN *has her back to* VICTORIA's *handbag. Her body shields the bag from* VICTORIA's *sight.*)

VICTORIA: But why? Why have you done it? You've trapped your friends down there as well as mine!

KAFTAN: I shall open it when Mr. Klieg has completed our plans. Meanwhile, it is better that they remain undisturbed. If you touch those controls . . . I shall have to kill you.

(*The Cybermat silently emerges from* VICTORIA's *handbag.*)

11. THE CYBER TOMB.

JAMIE: You know Doctor, I've a feeling that that man's planned it all. He knew that control wouldn't open the hatch.

THE DOCTOR: So did I, Jamie.

JAMIE: You knew, Doctor?

THE DOCTOR: I wanted to know what he was up to.

KLIEG: Now you know, Doctor.

PARRY: We know nothing. This is the action of a lunatic.

KLIEG: Lunatic? Not at all, Professor. A necessary detail, that's all.

PARRY: But why?

KLIEG: Logic, my dear Professor, logic and power!
On Earth, the Brotherhood of Logicians is
the greatest Man-intelligence ever
assembled. But that's not enough by itself,
we need power. Power to put our ability
into action. The Cybermen have this power.
I have come here to find it and use it.

PARRY: So that was your motive in financing my
expedition?

KLIEG: Precisely! Your complete lack of . . .
administration made it ideal for our
purpose.

THE DOCTOR: You think the Cybermen will help you?

KLIEG: Of course. I shall be their resurrector.
Look!

(*He points to the cells. Slowly, one by
one, the Cybermen begin to break free
from their cells. Huge, monstrous, silver beings. Emotionless. Ruthless.
Terrifying.*)

12. THE CONTROL ROOM.

(*The Cybermat is now completely out
of the bag. It begins to move along the
table towards* KAFTAN. VICTORIA *sees
it and backs away slightly.*)

KAFTAN: Keep still.

VICTORIA: Behind you . . . that thing . . . it's come
alive.

KAFTAN: You are so simple. You don't really expect to take me in with a trick like that.

VICTORIA: It's true. Look!

KAFTAN: Will nothing keep you still?

VICTORIA: Will you please look!

KAFTAN: If I have any more trouble from you I shall have to take drastic steps . . .

VICTORIA: Why won't you believe me?

KAFTAN: You don't think we can allow a little girl like you to interfere with our plans!

(*The Cybermat moves along the table towards* KAFTAN's *arm. It suddenly leaps onto her shoulder.* KAFTAN *screams and staggers back. She drops the gun.* VICTORIA *rushes forward, grasps the Cybermat and flings it to the ground. She tries desperately to revive* KAFTAN *but to no avail. She goes over to the control board, but does not know what to do. She goes over to the main door, and steps over the shattered Cybermat. She jumps as one of its antennae twitches purposefully.*)

VICTORIA: Captain Hopper!

13. *THE CYBER TOMB.*

(*The group of Cybermen move to-*

*wards one of the cells which is larger
than the rest, and form a semicircle
round it. One of the Cybermen steps
up to the cell and turns round towards
the others. One by one they all raise
their right arms in silent assent. The
Cyberman at the cell face then operates
bolts on the side of the cell and swings
back the membrane. Inside we see a
giant figure from which the frost is
now almost completely melted. Slowly
the figure begins to emerge from the
cell. The Cyberman who opened the
cell starts to offer his assistance, then
draws back in awe. The semicircle
also draws back a little and they bow
their heads. The Cyber-leader rises to
his full height. We now see that his
head is of an entirely different shape.
It is more bulbous and the top is
translucent, allowing sight of the crea-*
ture's enormous brain.)

JAMIE: What is it?

THE DOCTOR: I think it's their leader . . . their controller,
Jamie.

(KLIEG *walks alone up to the leader.
Hesitantly at first and then with growing confidence, he speaks.*)

KLIEG: I . . . am Klieg . . . Eric Klieg . . . I have
brought you back to life. We of the
Logicians have planned this. You are alive

because of us. Now will you help us?

(*The* CYBER CONTROLLER *does not react to this.* KLIEG *goes nearer.*)

We need your power, you need our mass intelligence. Are you listening?

(*There is still no reaction from the* CYBER CONTROLLER.)

Do you understand me? Now that I have released you . . .

(*The* CYBER CONTROLLER *seizes* KLIEG's *arm and he screams out in agony.*)

. . . aaaaaaaargh! Let me go. I set you free. It was our . . .

CYBER
CONTROLLER: You – belong – to – us. You – shall – be – like – us.

1. THE CYBER TOMB.

CONTROLLER: You – belong – to – us. You – shall – be – like – us.

(KLIEG *lies injured, on the floor, bewildered by the turn of events.*)

PARRY: How did you know that we would come to release you? You could have remained frozen for ever.

CONTROLLER: The – humanoid – mind. You – are – inquisitive.

THE DOCTOR: Ah, I see . . . a trap . . . a very special sort of trap, too.

PARRY: What do you mean – special trap?

THE DOCTOR: Don't you see – they only wanted superior intellects – that's why they made the trap so complicated.

CONTROLLER: We – knew – that – somebody – like – you – would – come – to – our – planet – someday.

THE DOCTOR: Yes and we have done exactly as you calculated, haven't we?

CONTROLLER: Now – you – belong – to – us.

2. *THE CONTROL ROOM.*

(KAFTAN *is still on the floor.* VICTORIA *rushes in followed by* HOPPER *and* CALLUM.)

VICTORIA: Now! Quick! Find the opening device. I don't know which it is.

HOPPER: Now, hold on. I'm not pulling any levers until I know what this is all about.

CALLUM: Don't reckon we should have left the rocket Captain. I can't see much wrong here.

VICTORIA: Not much wrong . . . are you blind, the pair of you?

(*She goes over to the hatch.*)

What about this then?

CALLUM: I can't see any change, Vic.

VICTORIA: That's just it. They're down there now.

(KAFTAN *stirs, opens an eye and sees the others.*)

HOPPER: Well then, why close the hatch on them? It don't make sense, Vic.

VICTORIA: I didn't. And please stop calling me 'Vic'. *She* closed the hatch.

(VICTORIA *indicates* KAFTAN.)

HOPPER: Oh, did she now?

VICTORIA: Now look, are you going to help me or not? They're probably freezing to death down there. If you're not going to help me, I'm going to pull every one of those levers on that board and see what happens.

HOPPER: Now I wouldn't do that, Vic. Come on Jim, we'd better do as she says.

CALLUM: Yeah.

(*The three of them cluster round the control panel.*)

HOPPER: O.K. now, were you here when they opened it all up?

VICTORIA: Yes.

(KAFTAN *opens her eyes again behind them.*)

HOPPER: Well come on – you must have some idea!

VICTORIA: I don't know, I wasn't looking. Oh, I think it's one of those levers down there.

(*She indicates the left hand side of the board.*)

CALLUM: She thinks!

> (VICTORIA *glares at him. The men begin examining the controls at the end of the board.*)

> 3. *THE CYBER TOMB.*

> (*The Cybermen are conferring at one end.* THE DOCTOR, PARRY, JAMIE, KLIEG *and* TOBERMAN *are at the other end of the tombs.*)

JAMIE: Can we not make a run for it, Doctor?

THE DOCTOR: No, no, we wouldn't even reach the ladder. It's too risky.

PARRY: What can we do?

THE DOCTOR: We'll play for time, watch for our chance. Leave it to me.

> (*He steps over to the* CYBER CONTROLLER *and clears his throat.*)

Ah-hem! Excuse me, may I ask a question? Why did you submit yourself to freezing?

> (*The* CYBER CONTROLLER *comes up to* THE DOCTOR *and looks closely at him.* THE DOCTOR *flinches away.*)

You don't have to answer that if you don't want to.

CONTROLLER: To – survive. Our – history – computer – has – full – details – of – you.

(*He points to* THE DOCTOR *and* JAMIE.)

THE DOCTOR: Oh. How?

CONTROLLER: We – know – of – your – intelligence.

THE DOCTOR: Oh, thank you very much – ah yes, the lunar surface.

CONTROLLER: Our – machinery – had – stopped – and – our – supply – of – replacements – been – depleted.

THE DOCTOR: So that's why you attacked the moonbase.

CONTROLLER: You – had – destroyed – our – first – planet – and – we – were – becoming – extinct.

JAMIE: What difference does capturing us make? You'll still become extinct.

CONTROLLER: We – will – survive. We – will – survive. Now – you – will – help – us.

PARRY: What makes you think we are going to help you?

(*He points to* KLIEG.)

That murderer doesn't speak for us.

CONTROLLER: You – will – become – the – first – of – a – new – race – of – Cybermen. You – will – return – to – the – Earth – and – control – it.

PARRY: Never, never!

CONTROLLER: Everything – we – decide – is – carried – out. There – are – no – mistakes.

JAMIE: A new race of Cybermen, but . . . but we're humans. We're not like you.

CONTROLLER: You – will – be.

> (JAMIE *decides to escape. He runs towards the passage leading to the escape ladder.*)

PARRY: Oh no . . . no . . . no. Keep away . . . keep away. Keep away from me.

4. *A Passage within the Cyber Tomb.*

> (JAMIE *runs to the ladder and starts to climb. Suddenly a Cyberman fires at* JAMIE *with his gun, and* JAMIE *collapses to the floor.* TOBERMAN *grapples with a Cyberman. At first it looks as if his giant strength is prevailing, but the Cyberman lifts* TOBERMAN *off the ground and throws him across the floor.*)

5. *The Cyber Tomb.*

> (THE DOCTOR *and* PARRY *are held in the Cybermen's vice-like grip.*)

THE DOCTOR: If only you'd let go of me, I'd stand still.

PARRY: Please, please . . . please let me go. Please, please . . . let me go, please.

THE DOCTOR: If you would let go of me, I would stand still
. . . You're breaking my arm!

CONTROLLER: To – struggle – is – futile.

(*The Cybermen carry their prisoners
towards the honeycomb of cells.*)

6. *THE CONTROL ROOM.*

(CALLUM *and* HOPPER *are crouched
down by the control console.* CALLUM
*has removed a board from the controls
and is examining the controls from
underneath.*)

HOPPER: You sure that's the one?

CALLUM: Yeah, yeah . . . yeah it's the only one it
could be. Yeah . . . it leads up to . . . that
one there.

(*Behind them* KAFTAN *has sat up. She
looks round. She sees the gun on the
floor by the hatch, and starts to move
towards it.* HOPPER *and* CALLUM *get to
their feet.*)

VICTORIA: Please *hurry*, Captain Hopper.

(*She moves forward to grasp the lever.*)

HOPPER: Keep back will you – leave this to me. Jim,
stand by the power cut off.

CALLUM: Power . . .? Yeah, yeah.

(*He stands at the other end of the board, his hand on a large power switch.* HOPPER *looks round at* VICTORIA.)

HOPPER: Stand back will you? Just in case we got the wrong one.

(VICTORIA *moves back nervously. The men stand by to pull the levers.*)

KAFTAN: Don't move.

(*The others react. They turn round.* KAFTAN *is facing them, gun in hand.*)

Raise your hands.

HOPPER: Now look here, lady . . .

(*He steps forward.*)

KAFTAN: I shall kill you.

(*She raises the gun in both hands and sights it.* HOPPER *stands still and raises his hands.*)

HOPPER: Well, your own men are down there, remember. What are you doing this for?

KAFTAN: Move away from that control board – over here.

(*She indicates the side of the room opposite the hatch.*)

I shall open the hatch when Klieg gives the signal.

HOPPER: Well, why close it in the first place?

KAFTAN: Klieg must remain undisturbed. Your friends will not escape from there – and you will not interfere.

> (*She is moving round them in a circle, towards the control panel. As she moves, her foot comes up against the disabled Cybermat. She freezes, unsure of what it is, but afraid to look down in case the men jump her.* VICTORIA *sees the Cybermat, and seizes her chance. She screams.* KAFTAN *starts, looks down, sees the Cybermat and jumps back in terror.* CALLUM *and* HOPPER *spring forward, and disarm her.*)

HOPPER: Watch her Jim. If she moves – blast her!

> (*He looks at* VICTORIA.)

CALLUM: Right.

HOPPER: You scream real good, Vic – thanks a lot!

VICTORIA: Please, the hatch.

HOPPER: O.K., we'll take a risk . . . Stand by.

> (*He pulls the lever. The grinding noise starts, and the heavy hatch cover*

swings open. VICTORIA *goes over and looks down, followed by* HOPPER *and* CALLUM. *They listen.*)

VICTORIA: It's very quiet down there.

HOPPER: Yeah . . . too quiet!

VICTORIA: Something must have happened.

HOPPER: How long have they been down there?

(VICTORIA *looks at her watch.*)

VICTORIA: Oh, about an hour.

HOPPER: That's too long. I'm going down.

(*He swings his feet over the edge of the hatch. As he does he catches sight of something. He points to* CALLUM's *belt.*)

Hey Jim, what are those bombs loaded with?

CALLUM: Er . . . Smoke.

HOPPER: Great, give us a couple, will you?

CALLUM: Yeah, sure.

HOPPER: C'mon, c'mon!

CALLUM: Yeah, yeah.

(*He hands* HOPPER *two bombs.*)

HOPPER: O.K., here we go.

VICTORIA: I'm coming too.

HOPPER: Later, maybe. Not this trip.

VICTORIA: Who'd be a woman?

HOPPER: How would you know, honey? You'd better stay up here. We don't know what's going on down there!

(*He disappears down the hatch.* VICTORIA *makes a face.*)

VICTORIA: Is he always like that?

(CALLUM *grins.*)

CALLUM: Most of the time Vic, yeah.

(VICTORIA *gives him a furious glance and settles down to wait.*)

7. *THE CYBER TOMB.*

(*The Cybermen are conferring at the end of the room by the control panel.* THE DOCTOR, JAMIE, PARRY *and* KLIEG *are grouped together with the still unconscious* TOBERMAN. *The* CYBER CONTROLLER *and a* CYBERMAN *come over to them and address* KLIEG.)

CONTROLLER: We – have – decided – how – you – will – be – used.

(KLIEG's *hopes rise.*)

KLIEG: Yes?

CONTROLLER: You – are – a – Logician. Our – race – is – also – logical. You – will – be – the – leader – of – the – new – race.

KLIEG: You will listen to my proposals then?

CONTROLLER: Yes. We – will – listen. But – first – you – will – be – altered.

(*Realisation dawns on* KLIEG'*s horror-struck face.*)

KLIEG: Altered . . .?

CONTROLLER: You – have – fear? We – will – eliminate – fear – from – your – brain. Yes – you – will – be – the – first.

(KLIEG *draws back in terror. The* CYBERMAN *turns to* PARRY.)

CONTROLLER: And – you – will – be – the – next.

PARRY: Me . . . no . . . *no*!!

(*The* CYBERMAN *grabs hold of* PARRY'*s arm.* PARRY *screams in pain.*)

CONTROLLER: You – will – be – like – us.

8. *A PASSAGE WITHIN THE CYBER TOMB.*

(HOPPER *is crouched down, listening to this. He unclips one of the smoke bombs and holds it ready.*)

9. THE CYBER TOMB.

CONTROLLER: To – die – is – unnecessary. You – will – be – frozen – and – placed – in – our – tombs – until – we – are – ready – to – use – you. Your – lives – will – be – suspended. Prepare – the – tombs.

(*The* CYBER CONTROLLER *operates a control and around the edges of the open cells, which now contain the captives, frost begins to form. They immediately begin to shiver.*)

PARRY: They really mean it! They're going to freeze us.

JAMIE: Not me.

THE DOCTOR: Look Jamie, they're coming back!

(*He springs to his feet and faces the Cybermen. They start to move threateningly towards him. Without warning, smoke bombs burst on the ground near the Cybermen and they reel around in confusion.*)

HOPPER: Come on you guys – run for it!

10. A PASSAGE WITHIN THE CYBER TOMB.

(*The former captives reach the passage.* JAMIE *is helping* PARRY.)

THE DOCTOR: Is he all right?

(*They reach a fork in the passage.*)

JAMIE: I think so. Which way? I can't remember.

THE DOCTOR: That way.

JAMIE: Are you sure?

THE DOCTOR: No, I'm not sure, but try it. I'll join you in a moment.

> (KLIEG *staggers along a passage followed by* HOPPER, *who is anxiously looking behind him.* THE DOCTOR *goes over to* HOPPER. KLIEG *halts, looks at the fork, and takes the left-hand one.*)

THE DOCTOR: We've got to stop them.

HOPPER: Block off this tunnel, perhaps?

THE DOCTOR: No, no, no, we can't do that. The hatch . . . we must get there first. Come on.

> (TOBERMAN *stumbles along blinded by the thickening smoke. He feels his way along the walls of the passage. A Cyberman looms out of the smoke.* TOBERMAN *turns to run, but the Cyberman reaches out and grasps him by the shoulder.* TOBERMAN *turns and delivers a massive swipe, which simply bounces off the Cyberman. Two more Cybermen approach. The one* TOBER-

MAN *has been fighting raises his arm.
A spark jumps from his finger and
strikes* TOBERMAN *on the forehead.*
TOBERMAN *staggers and blinks but
does not go down. Again the Cyberman fires. The smoke clears and we
see that the Cyberman* TOBERMAN *has
been fighting is the* CYBER CON-
TROLLER.)

CONTROLLER: This – humanoid – is – powerful. We – will
– use – him. Prepare – him.

(*Two Cybermen pick up* TOBERMAN
and carry him away.)

11. THE LADDER.

(*Further down the passageway by the
ladder, are* JAMIE, PARRY *and* HOPPER.
JAMIE's *progress is being hampered by*
PARRY.)

HOPPER: Hurry up can't you? For Pete's sake get a
move on.

(HOPPER *helps* JAMIE *to pull up the
barely conscious* PARRY. *With diffi-
culty, they reach the top.*)

PARRY: I . . . I . . . can't breathe.

JAMIE: Victoria!

12. *THE CONTROL ROOM.*

(VICTORIA *and* CALLUM *look over the rim of the hatch.*)

VICTORIA: Jamie! Look at that smoke.

JAMIE (*oov*): Victoria. Come on Mr. Parry, come on, quick!

(CALLUM *runs over and helps* JAMIE *out, who in turn helps* PARRY *out.* HOPPER's *head shows above the rim. He looks down.*)

CALLUM: Stand back.

HOPPER: The Cybermen. They're right behind us.

13. *THE LADDER.*

(THE DOCTOR *is climbing. Just below is a* CYBERMAN, *steadily gaining on him.*)

14. *THE CONTROL ROOM.*

(HOPPER *climbs out of the hatch.*)

HOPPER: As soon as the Doctor is up, slam down the hatch!

CALLUM: O.K.

(CALLUM *runs over to the control panel.* THE DOCTOR's *head appears over the*

rim of the hatch. HOPPER *gives him a
helping hand.* HOPPER *calls over to*
CALLUM.)

HOPPER: Stand by!

            (THE DOCTOR *suddenly cries out in
            pain.*)

THE DOCTOR: Oh . . . Aaargh! He's got my leg!

            (CALLUM'*s hand hovers indecisively
            over the closing controls.* THE DOCTOR'*s
            hands desperately grip the rim of the
            hatch.* HOPPER *leans over and grasps*
            THE DOCTORS'*s arms.*)

JAMIE: Doctor . . . come on.

THE DOCTOR: Oh . . . it's no use!

            (THE DOCTOR'*s hands start to slip. The
            head and shoulders of the Cyberman
            appear behind him – its hands clasping*
            THE DOCTOR *firmly round the shoul-
            ders.* VICTORIA *looks round in desper-
            ation and, seeing the open flask of
            coffee, picks it up and runs over to the
            hatch. She flings the contents into the
            Cyberman's face.*)

HOPPER: Jim! Close the hatch!

JAMIE: Victoria!

            (*The Cyberman releases his hold on*

THE DOCTOR, *who falls into the room, and grabs* VICTORIA*'s arms instead.* VICTORIA *screams and drops the flask.* CALLUM *operates the closing mechanism. The gears grind and the heavy lid of the hatch starts to close on the Cyberman. He raises one arm, and for a moment it looks as if he is strong enough to stop it.* JAMIE *is trying to pull* VICTORIA *free, but the Cyberman's other arm is still holding her. The Cyberman's arm bends as the full weight of the lid is felt and he releases his grip on* VICTORIA. *The lid continues to close.*)

CALLUM: Got him!

(*There is a tremendous clanging sound as the Cyberman below hits the now closed lid of the hatch. At each blow we see a dent appear in its surface. The blows stop. Everyone stands transfixed for a moment.* JAMIE *goes to* VICTORIA *who is nearly fainting.*)

VICTORIA: It was horrible – it was so strong!

(JAMIE *holds her.*)

JAMIE: It's all right, Victoria. You're all right now.

PARRY: That was a near thing. Is anyone missing?

THE DOCTOR: Yes . . .

HOPPER: Klieg and Toberman – they're still down there!

15. *A Passage within the Cyber Tomb.*

(KLIEG *has found a niche in the passage. He squeezes in, out of sight, just as three Cybermen come up, led by the* CYBER CONTROLLER. *They march past him one by one as he presses his face close to the rock. They halt just past him and look up the ladder.*)

CONTROLLER: The – humanoid – has – escaped.

CYBERMAN: Yes.

CONTROLLER: Guard – the – passageway.

CYBERMAN: Yes.

(*The Cybermen march off.*)

16. *The Ladder.*

(KLIEG *reaches the top. He raises his fist to knock, but is frightened to do so in case the Cyberman below hear him. He agonises for a moment and then softly knocks and listens.*)

17. THE CONTROL ROOM.

(Two muffled knocks are heard coming from the hatch. There is a pause and then two more knocks.)

PARRY: Don't open it! It may be the Cybermen.

THE DOCTOR: No, no – it's too soft. It must be Toberman and Klieg.

HOPPER: Ah, you're crazy!

PARRY: You're right! We can't leave them down there, even if they are killers.

JAMIE: Well, they're both probably frozen solid by now.

(There are two more muffled knocks.)

KAFTAN: You must let them up – they must be saved.

THE DOCTOR: Yes, they're more dangerous down there than they are up here.

(HOPPER doesn't understand this, but nevertheless he draws his gun to cover the hatch.)

HOPPER: What . . .? O.K. Jim!

CALLUM: Right.

(JAMIE grasps one of the stools and stands on the other side of the hatch. The knocking is heard again.)

HOPPER: O.K. Let her go!

THE DOCTOR: Excuse me please.

> (THE DOCTOR *moves to one side as* CALLUM *works the lever. The others watch tensely as the lid slowly opens.* JAMIE *and* HOPPER *raise their weapons.* KLIEG *bursts out and collapses on the floor.* HOPPER *lowers his weapon and goes over to the hatch, looking down for* TOBERMAN. KAFTAN *runs across.*)

KLIEG: Close it . . . close it quick!

KAFTAN: Eric – where's Toberman?

KLIEG: They've got him.

> (KLIEG *is nearly hysterical.* HOPPER *nods to* CALLUM *who operates the closing sequence. The hatch grinds shut.* THE DOCTOR *comes over to* KLIEG.)

THE DOCTOR: You still think you can form an alliance with the Cybermen, Mr. Klieg?

KLIEG: If I'd only been in a stronger position to bargain with them.

PARRY: You must be out of your mind, Klieg.

HOPPER: You're not in any position to bargain with anybody, right now.

> (*He looks at* PARRY.)

What are we going to do with him?

PARRY: I'd feel much happier if they weren't left in here.

THE DOCTOR: Well, what about the testing room? There's only one door. They can't get out.

PARRY: That's a good idea. They'll be quite safe in there. Callum.

PARRY: Right . . . Mr. Klieg? Miss Kaftan?

(HOPPER *nods to* CALLUM, *who leads off* KLIEG *and* KAFTAN.)

HOPPER: Now, if I don't get back to the rocket, we're not going to take off inside a week.

PARRY: We'll come with you.

HOPPER: I've told you before, not 'til I'm operational again. I'll let you know when that is.

(*He exits. As he does, he passes the hatch.*)

I don't think you'll have any more trouble with your friends down there.

THE DOCTOR: We shall see.

18. *THE CYBER TOMB.*

(*The Cybermen are standing in a semi-circle around the* CYBER CON-TROLLER, *who is by the control board.*)

CONTROLLER: Release – the – Cybermats! We – will – use – the – power – of – Cybernetics.

(*The Cybermen go over to two large cupboards set in the wall, open them and take out three Cybermats.*)

Activate – them. The – brain – of – this – humanoid – will – be – their – target.

(*The* CYBER CONTROLLER *turns and signals to a Cyberman at the control desk. The latter operates a lever.*)

Now . . . These – Cybermats – are – dormant – through – lack – of – use. Inspect – them!

(*The Cybermen pick them up, turn them over and make some adjustments.*)

19. THE TESTING ROOM.

(KLIEG *is sleeping,* KAFTAN *keeping watch by him. She goes over to the Cybergun and examines it. She dislodges a loose piece of metal and the clatter wakes* KLIEG, *who sits up.*)

KLIEG: What's that?

KAFTAN: Just me.

(KLIEG *grunts irritably and turns to go back to sleep.*)

KLIEG: Oh, be quiet!

KAFTAN: Sleep later. Look at this.

(KLIEG *raises himself up again.*)

KLIEG: What is it?

KAFTAN: It's one of the weapons they were testing. Look here's the connection.

KLIEG: Let me see.

(*Sleep forgotten,* KLIEG *scrambles to his feet, and goes over to examine the Cybergun.*)

Oh yes, you're right. It's a Cybergun! Take a look at that control. See that everything is switched off.

KAFTAN: Right.

(*She goes over to the control console and looks over it.*)

All the sequences show negative.

KLIEG: Good.

(*He feels in a pouch in the side of his clothes and brings out a set of jeweller's tools. He starts to dismantle the weapon.*)

Now they will have to listen!

20. *THE CYBER TOMB.*

(*The Cybermen have finished making adjustments to the Cybermats. They are aligning them on* TOBERMAN.)

CYBERMAN: The – Cybermats – are – ready.

CONTROLLER: Stand – clear!

(*The two Cybermen stand well clear of* TOBERMAN *and form the Cybermats into a horseshoe around him.*)

Now!

(*He pulls a lever. A low whine begins, rising gradually in pitch. The* CYBER CONTROLLER *selects a control knob near the lever and turns it. The whine rises even higher in pitch and becomes staccato, giving out a Morse code-like series of noises, clearly a control signal.* TOBERMAN, *who is fully conscious, is clearly terrified, his face covered in sweat.*)

21. *THE TESTING ROOM.*

(KLIEG *is taking aim with the Cyber-gun.* KAFTAN *moves back nervously as* KLIEG *points the gun at a metal panel*

*on the other side of the room. He
presses a button. There is a flash, and
a curl of smoke rises from a newly
formed hole in the target.)*

KLIEG: Excellent! A small X-ray laser.

(He examines the panel in wonder.)

KAFTAN: What are you going to do now?

KLIEG: Take command of course, what do you
think? With this, I shall be able to deal with
those people in there.

*(KLIEG has his back to the panel. He
and KAFTAN do not notice a Cybermat
crawling through the burnt hole in the
panel.)*

KAFTAN: Never mind about them. The important
thing for us is to control the Cybermen.

KLIEG: Yes I know . . . but . . .

KAFTAN: Isn't it, Eric?

KLIEG: You haven't been down there, you haven't
seen those . . . vile things.

KAFTAN: You're not scared are you?

KLIEG: We have completely underestimated their
power.

KAFTAN: But this time we have the power. At least,
you do.

(KLIEG *looks mystified.*)

The gun, Eric, the gun. You have the
Cybermen's own weapon – this laser – to
turn against them. Now they will have to
obey. If they refuse, we shall destroy the
opening device and seal them up in their
tomb for ever. Now do you understand?

KLIEG: Yes, yes you're right. I am invulnerable
with this. I shall be master.

KAFTAN: Come. Let us deal with these people first.

(*Having half heard* KLIEG's *last sen-
tence, and because he is not following
her,* KAFTAN *turns back to him.*)

Eric?

(*He is talking to himself and does not
immediately hear her.*)

KLIEG: Master. The supreme moment of my life. It
was logical.

KAFTAN: Eric, we have work to do.

KLIEG: Yes, yes – of course, but hardly work –
more a pleasure.

KAFTAN: What?

KLIEG: A pleasure – to get this on that Doctor and
his companions. The others are of no
consequence, but he will make a most
precise target.

(*The antennae on the Cybermat's head twitch.*)

22. *THE CYBER TOMB*.

CONTROLLER: Enough! These – humanoids – are – not – like – us. They – still – have – fear. Place – the – Cybermats – on – the – runway.

(*The Cybermen lift the three Cyber-mats and carry them to a cupboard which reveals a chute leading upwards, just wide enough to take the body of a Cybermat. The first one is placed on the chute.*)

Cybermats – will – attack!

23. *THE CONTROL ROOM*.

(VICTORIA *is half asleep.* JAMIE *is asleep by the table, along with both* THE DOCTOR *and* PARRY. CALLUM *is asleep, sprawled out on the floor, propped up by the hatch.* THE DOCTOR *suddenly wakes. He blinks, stretches and notices* VICTORIA. *He scrambles to his feet and goes over to join her, yawning as he does so.*)

THE DOCTOR: I'm on your side, remember. Hey, why didn't you wake me? I should have been on watch half an hour ago.

VICTORIA: I thought you should rest.

THE DOCTOR: Why me?

VICTORIA: No reason really.

(*She flushes, slightly embarrassed.* THE DOCTOR's *face breaks into a smile.*)

THE DOCTOR: Oh, I think I know – is it because I'm . . .?

VICTORIA: Well . . . if you are 450 years old, you need a great deal of sleep.

THE DOCTOR: Well that's very considerate of you Victoria, but . . . between you and me I'm . . . I'm really quite lively actually – all things being considered.

(*He sits beside her.*)

Are you happy with us, Victoria?

VICTORIA: Yes, I am. At least, I would be if my father were here.

THE DOCTOR: Yes I know, I know.

VICTORIA: I wonder what he would have thought if he could see me now.

THE DOCTOR: You miss him very much, don't you?

VICTORIA: It's only when I close my eyes. I can still see him standing there, before those horrible Dalek creatures came to the house. He was a very kind man. I shall never forget him . . . never.

THE DOCTOR: No, of course you won't, but, you know, the memory of him won't always be a sad one.

VICTORIA: I think it will. You can't understand, being so ancient.

THE DOCTOR: Eh?

VICTORIA: I mean old.

THE DOCTOR: Oh!

VICTORIA: You probably can't remember your family.

THE DOCTOR: Oh yes I can, when I want to. And that's the point really; I have to really *want* to, to bring them back in front of my eyes – the rest of the time they . . . they sleep in my mind and I forget. And so will you.

(VICTORIA *looks doubtful.*)

Oh yes, you will. You'll find there's so much else to think about, to remember. Our lives are different to . . . anybody else's, that's the exciting thing. Nobody in the Universe can do what we're doing . . . You must get some sleep and let this poor old man stay awake.

(*A small hatch slowly opens near the floor and the first Cybermat enters the room. Two more follow and they advance into the room in jerks, towards the table. One goes up to* THE DOCTOR *and brushes his foot. He starts and hurriedly moves his foot out of reach.*)

THE DOCTOR: Jamie, Victoria, Callum! Wake up! Wake up!

(*The others stir and wake.*)

JAMIE: Mmmm . . . what?

VICTORIA: What is it?

(*One of the Cybermats reaches the still sleeping* CALLUM *and begins crawling up his chest.*)

THE DOCTOR: Callum. *Callum!*

(CALLUM *starts to wake up.*)

VICTORIA: One of those terrible things again!

(CALLUM *wakes up and sees the Cybermat on his chest.*)

THE DOCTOR: Don't . . . move. Callum, don't move.

(THE DOCTOR *edges nearer and with one quick movement brushes the Cybermat off* CALLUM's *shoulder. The Cybermat falls to the ground on its back. It tries to right itself, and eventually does so.*)

THE DOCTOR: Now get back to the controls all of you. Steady . . . don't make any sudden movements.

(*They back away slowly.* THE DOCTOR *turns to* PARRY.)

Parry, Parry. Wake up, Parry. Wake up. Wake up!

(PARRY *opens his eyes and, with horror, sees the Cybermats.*)

Don't panic, come back with us. Steady.

(PARRY *slowly gets to his feet.*)

Now we'll all go in the other room and lock them out.

(*They back away towards the Recharging Room door.* VICTORIA *turns and screams. There are three more Cybermats coming out of that door.*)

CALLUM: Let's get out of here – the main doors!

(*He moves towards them,* VICTORIA *and* JAMIE *close on his heels.*)

JAMIE: No, look!

(*Another Cybermat is coming in through the main entrance. They back away to the control board.*)

VICTORIA: Oh, Doctor! We're trapped.

(*The Cybermats are making a chatter-
ing noise. Every so often their antennae
move towards other Cybermats. They
are communicating with each other.*)

THE DOCTOR: Back against the controls – everybody.

(*They back to the control panel. The
Cybermats stop for a moment, un-
decided which direction their victims
have taken. One of them senses the
presence of* THE DOCTOR *and* PARRY
*and starts angrily bleeping. It turns
towards them.* THE DOCTOR *sees a
length of stout cable running between
the two consoles and, in a flash, pulls
out a pair of wire clippers.*)

Here, give me a hand – quick!

(*He cuts the cable loose.*)

Lay this down on the ground. Come on.

JAMIE: Will it hold then, Doctor?

(PARRY *begins to catch on. He lays it
down around them.* THE DOCTOR *has
jammed the two ends into two sockets
on the console.*)

THE DOCTOR: Come on!

CALLUM: Let's blast the filthy things . . .

(*He fires three times. One of the Cyber-mats is hit, and turns on its side, slowly dying.*)

THE DOCTOR: You're wasting your time, there are too many of them. Now, do as I say, come back.

(CALLUM *obeys. The Cybermats advance towards the cable, their intermittent humming getting louder. As they approach the cable their movements become erratic. They bump into each other and begin to run around in circles.*)

There you are, you see.

PARRY: What are those creatures?

(*The Cybermats are now almost completely out of control. Some have curled up and smoke is issuing from them. Others are still feebly moving around in circles.*)

THE DOCTOR: Well, they're a . . . they're a form of . . . of metallic life. They home on human brain waves and attack.

VICTORIA: Ergh! Are they safe now?

THE DOCTOR: Oh yes, quite safe now. The power cable generated an electrical field and confused their tiny metal minds. You might almost say they had a complete metal breakdown.

(JAMIE *groans at the pun.*)

JAMIE: Oh!

THE DOCTOR: I'm so sorry, Jamie.

VICTORIA: What about Klieg and Kaftan? They pro-
             bably attacked them, as well.

PARRY: The testing room!

THE DOCTOR: Now come on! Now, mind your feet.

> (*As* THE DOCTOR *and the others are
> about to leave the Control Room,*
> KLIEG *enters. He is holding a gun in
> his hand.*)

KLIEG: Most ingenious, Doctor! Now let's see what
             you can do against this.

> (KLIEG *raises the gun and fires.*)

1. THE CONTROL ROOM.

(KLIEG *shoots* CALLUM, *who falls to the ground in agony, clutching his shoulder.* PARRY *rushes to help him, but is waved back by* KLIEG.)

KLIEG: Keep back. Your gun.

PARRY: You've killed him, you murderer!

KLIEG: No, he's fortunate, I spared him.

JAMIE: You mean you missed him.

KLIEG: Silence! I could have destroyed him if I'd wanted to. Shall I kill them now?

KAFTAN: No, no, that will not be necessary. I'm sure the Cybermen will have a good use for them. You will make excellent experimental specimens.

(KLIEG *smiles sardonically.* THE DOCTOR, PARRY, JAMIE *and* VICTORIA *are now lined up against the wall.* CALLUM *groans.*)

VICTORIA: Oh let me help him! Please.

(KLIEG *looks at* KAFTAN *who nods consent. He goes over to the control panel and begins the hatch opening sequence.*)

KLIEG: No tricks!

THE DOCTOR: You still think you can bargain with the Cybermen?

KLIEG: Certainly, and this time on our terms.

(*The grinding noise starts up, and the hatch slowly opens.* KLIEG *goes over to the hatch and calls down.*)

KLIEG: I wish to speak to the Controller.

(*He raises his voice.*)

I wish to speak to the Controller.

2. *THE CYBER TOMB.*

(*Some Cybermen are still grouped around the* CYBER CONTROLLER. *Others are standing by a bench opposite the control panel. The voice of* KLIEG *echoes down the passage.*)

KLIEG (*oov*): I wish to speak to the Controller.

CONTROLLER: The – humanoids – must – first – be – destroyed. You – will – re-enter – cells – to – conserve – energy.

> (*The Cybermen start to enter the cells. The* CYBER CONTROLLER *indicates* TOBERMAN.)

CYBERMAN: He – is – now – prepared.

CONTROLLER: Release – him.

> (TOBERMAN *is released and comes forward. He is covered in a loose, white smock.*)

3. THE CONTROL ROOM.

KLIEG: They're coming.

> (*He turns to the others.*)

And now gentlemen, you will see how I shall use the power of the Cybermen.

THE DOCTOR: Use, maybe. But you'll never control the Cybermen.

> (*The* CYBER CONTROLLER's *head comes through the hatch.* KAFTAN *sees him first.*)

KAFTAN: Eric! Behind you!

(KLIEG *wheels round, the Cybergun in his hand.*)

KLIEG: Stop! You know what this can do to you.

(*The* CYBER CONTROLLER *stands still.*)

That's better. Now you are under my control. We know you must be revitalised or you will perish. If you agree to my terms, I shall let you survive.

CONTROLLER: I – will – listen.

(KAFTAN *comes up to* KLIEG *and whispers in his ear.*)

KAFTAN: Make them release Toberman.

JAMIE: If you think that they will listen to you, you're even dafter than I thought.

KLIEG: Silence! Sit down.

(*He turns back to the* CYBER CONTROLLER).

First . . . you release our man.

(*The* CYBER CONTROLLER *turns to face* TOBERMAN, *who has climbed into the room after him.* TOBERMAN *stares hard at him as if receiving a telepathic message and moves forward.*)

KAFTAN: Toberman, it is good that you are back. Watch them.

(TOBERMAN *nods and turns towards* THE DOCTOR *and the others.*)

JAMIE: Doctor, he seems er . . .

(THE DOCTOR *looks up sharply at* TOBERMAN.)

THE DOCTOR: Yes Jamie, yes.

(*The* CYBER CONTROLLER *starts to come forward.*)

KLIEG: Stay where you are. Now . . . do you agree to accept our plan.

THE DOCTOR: Plan?

KLIEG: The conquest of the Earth.

PARRY: What! You must be . . .

KLIEG: Silence! Your answer?

CONTROLLER: We – accept. We – will – give – you – some – of – our – power – devices.

KLIEG: Good. I knew an understanding could be reached. I shall let you be revitalized. To survive, it must be now. Come forward . . . slowly.

KAFTAN: Eric, be careful!

KLIEG: Leave this to me.

(*The* CYBER CONTROLLER *comes forward. Everyone shrinks back. He goes
out of the door leading to the Revitalization Room. Just before he leaves he
turns towards the group and to* TOBER-
MAN. THE DOCTOR *is very aware of
this.* PARRY *turns angrily on* KLIEG.)

PARRY: You are absolutely crazy to trust them.

KLIEG: You think so. Then perhaps you and your
colleagues had better join him. Go on . . .
go on.

(*He pushes* PARRY, THE DOCTOR *and*
JAMIE *out after the* CYBER CON-
TROLLER. VICTORIA *tries to go with
them but* KLIEG *pulls her back.*)

KLIEG: The girl stays with us.

(THE DOCTOR *and* JAMIE *both protest
vehemently.*)

If there is any trouble she is our hostage.
Close the hatch!

(*He addresses* TOBERMAN, *who does
not move.*)

KAFTAN: Go on, close it.

(TOBERMAN *moves behind* KLIEG *and
folds his arms, his features blank.*

Irritated by this, KAFTAN *closes the hatch herself.*)

4. *THE RECHARGING ROOM.*

(*The* CYBER CONTROLLER *is standing before the sarcophagus shape. He tries to climb into the form, but is too weak to make it.* THE DOCTOR, JAMIE *and* PARRY *enter.*)

JAMIE: He's too weak to get in.

THE DOCTOR: Quiet, Jamie.

(*He motions towards the* CYBER CONTROLLER *and goes up to him.*)

THE DOCTOR: You seem to be in trouble.

(*The* CYBER CONTROLLER *turns slowly to* THE DOCTOR. *His voice is slurring and he sounds weak.*)

CONTROLLER: The – energy – levels – are – low. We – will – survive. You – will – help – us. You – will – help – us.

(*His head droops. It is almost pathetic.*)

THE DOCTOR: Yes, yes, certainly. Jamie, Professor!

JAMIE: You don't mean to say you're actually going to help them?

PARRY: Surely not. You can't support these creatures.

THE DOCTOR: I think it best. Come on, come along. That's it . . . up . . .

(THE DOCTOR *helps the* CYBER CONTROLLER *into the form. He stands passively inside.*)

CONTROLLER: You – understand – the – machine?

THE DOCTOR: Yes – one moment.

(*He walks over to the control panel.*)

JAMIE: Have you taken leave of your senses? Now let's go and help Victoria.

THE DOCTOR: In a moment, Jamie. Now are you ready?

(THE DOCTOR *operates the controls. The lid of the sarcophagus starts to close. The Bio-projectors pulse with light and power, their nozzles swinging towards the form. As it closes, the* CYBER CONTROLLER'*s voice becomes just a slur.*)

CONTROLLER: We – will – survive. We . . . will . . . surrrrr . . .

(*The lid is now fully closed.*)

THE DOCTOR: Now then. Where would you rather have him, in or out of there?

(*He turns back to the control panel and examines it.*)

JAMIE: Oh! I see what you mean.

THE DOCTOR: Only we must make sure that he stays in there.

5. THE CONTROL ROOM.

VICTORIA: Do you really believe you can bargain with those terrible Cybermen?

KAFTAN: That is our concern, not yours.

VICTORIA: I'm talking to him, not you.

KLIEG: They will have to agree to our plan.

VICTORIA: What about the other weapon?

KLIEG: What other weapon?

VICTORIA: Well, I saw another one like that in that room over there.

(KLIEG *looks at* KAFTAN.)

KLIEG: Is that true?

KAFTAN: I don't know. We'd better make sure.

(*She goes towards the door.*)

KLIEG: No wait – that means that any one of them in there could . . .

KAFTAN: Yes, you're right, Eric.

KLIEG: We'd better wait here. If the Cyberman is aroused, we shall be ready for him. Now, stay well clear. Take no chances!

(KAFTAN *nods and goes over to the control panel.* TOBERMAN *impassively comes and stands by* KLIEG.)

6. *THE RECHARGING ROOM.*

(*The sarcophagus has been secured with two stout cables, and the revitalization process is now in full swing. The Bio-projectors are pulsing, lights are flashing, and smoke is curling up from the massive cables leading to the sarcophagus.*)

PARRY: Keep back – it's smoking.

(*The men stand and watch in awe – not knowing what will happen next.*)

JAMIE: I told you we shouldn't have touched it.

PARRY: Yes. Turn it off. It's out of control!

(PARRY *reaches out, but before he can reach the controls, they turn off by themselves.*)

PARRY: It's taken over!

THE DOCTOR: I think not. I think there must be some sort of internal timing mechanism.

(*He backs away nervously from the trapped* CYBER CONTROLLER.)

Jamie, I hope you made those ropes secure.

JAMIE: Oh, the King of the Beasties himself could na' get out of that one.

(*The sarcophagus begins to vibrate. There is the sound of heavy blows coming from inside. Cracks appear on the surface. There is a larger crash, plus the sound of rending metal. The gauntletted hand of the* CYBER CON-TROLLER *appears through one of the fractures.*)

THE DOCTOR: Jamie, remind me to give you a lesson in tying knots sometime.

(*The cracks spread. The whole upper lid splits and is flung contemptuously aside. The* CYBER CONTROLLER'*s head is flashing with power. His movements are once again vigorous and powerful. He bears down on the cringing humans. They back against the wall, bowing to his sheer size and force of presence.*)

CONTROLLER: You – will – remain – still.

(*A light starts to flash on the control panel and a buzzing noise begins.*)

7. *THE CONTROL ROOM.*

(*The buzzing noise continues.* TOBER-MAN's *eyes widen.* TOBERMAN *and* KLIEG *are standing by the door to the recharging room.*)

KLIEG: Stay here, and watch that door.

(*He turns to* KAFTAN.)

At least now we shall have some warning.

(*They sit.* KLIEG *puts down the Cyber-gun.*)

CALLUM: What do you two hope to gain from all this?

KLIEG: That does not concern you.

(*Without the others realising,* TOBER-MAN *is moving behind* KLIEG *and* KAFTAN. VICTORIA *can see him, but stays silent.*)

KAFTAN: Oh they might as well know, Eric. We are going to build a better world.

CALLUM: Better? Well who for?

(*Suddenly* KLIEG *realises that* TOBER-MAN *is standing behind him.*)

KLIEG: I told you to watch that door.

> (TOBERMAN *raises his arm and, as he does so, his sleeve falls back to reveal a Cyberman's arm. He chops* KLIEG *with a single blow.* KAFTAN *screams and* TOBERMAN *turns towards her, confused by her voice. The door opens and the* CYBER CONTROLLER *enters followed by* THE DOCTOR, PARRY *and* JAMIE. *The* CYBER CONTROLLER *picks up the Cybergun. He turns to* TOBERMAN.)

JAMIE: Victoria!

CONTROLLER: You – have – done – well.

> (VICTORIA *runs to* JAMIE *and* THE DOCTOR.)

KAFTAN: Toberman!

> (TOBERMAN *looks at her, confused.*)

CONTROLLER: Silence! He – is – now – under – our – control. Open – the – tombs.

KAFTAN: No! You have broken your promise.

CONTROLLER: Cybermen – do – not – promise. Such – ideas – have – no – value. Open!

KAFTAN: No!

> (The CYBER CONTROLLER *comes over*

to the control panel. KAFTAN *backs
away from him. He activates the opening controls. The gears start to grind
the hatch open, and he turns away.*
KAFTAN *quickly darts in and operates
the closing controls. The hatch starts
to close again. She takes* CALLUM's
gun from her belt. The CYBER CON-
TROLLER, *realising what she has done,
advances towards her.* KAFTAN *fires at
him, but the bullets have no effect.*)

CONTROLLER: That – gun – will – not – harm – me.

(KAFTAN *fires again. The* CYBER CON-
TROLLER *raises his gun and shoots*
KAFTAN. *She falls to the ground, her
body smouldering.* VICTORIA *screams.*
TOBERMAN *puts his hand to his head
and takes a step towards her. He is
confused and examines his hand in
awe. The* CYBER CONTROLLER *goes to
the control panel and re-activates the
opening controls.* THE DOCTOR *steps
to* TOBERMAN's *side.*)

THE DOCTOR: Look what they've done. You are not like
them. You're a man like us, you must help
us.

(*The* CYBER CONTROLLER *passes them
on his way to the hatch.*)

He has killed Kaftan – you must help us.

(*The* CYBER CONTROLLER *reaches the hatch and calls down into it.*)

CONTROLLER: You – will – report – to – the – surface.

(TOBERMAN *looks from* THE DOCTOR *to the* CYBER CONTROLLER. *He is confused. His arm jerks forwards, he is still uncertain of his power. He starts forward. The* CYBER CONTROLLER *is still looking down the hatch, waiting for the other Cybermen.* TOBERMAN *advances, striking the weapon from the* CYBER CONTROLLER'*s hand.* JAMIE *picks it up. The* CYBER CONTROLLER *swings with his arm, narrowly missing* TOBERMAN. *The tremendous power of the blow completely shattering the control panel.* TOBERMAN *roars in rage and strikes the* CYBER CONTROLLER *again. This time he is damaged by the force of the blow, and smoke starts to rise from his chest. The* CYBER CONTROLLER'*s movements become jerky. With another roar,* TOBERMAN *moves in for the kill. He bends down, picks up the* CYBER CONTROLLER *and flings him against another control panel.* THE DOCTOR *and the others watch in the background, unable to help. The* CYBER CONTROLLER *is lying against the broken control panel, apparently dead. Smoke still curls up from his body.* TOBERMAN *comes and stands over him looking down with grim triumph.* THE DOCTOR *suddenly looks over to the hatch as another Cyberman starts to appear through it.*)

THE DOCTOR: Jamie, the hatch . . . The gun Jamie!

(JAMIE *runs across to the hatch, firing the Cybergun. The Cyberman stands in the hatch, smoke pouring from its mouth. It jerks and hangs limply over the edge of the opening.* JAMIE *runs forward and tips it back down the ladder. There is a distant crashing noise, metal on metal, as the Cyberman hits the floor of the tomb.*)

JAMIE: There's another one, Doctor!

(*He shoots again down the hatchway. There is the sound of another Cyberman crashing to the floor far beneath, then silence.*)

THE DOCTOR: Are there any more?

JAMIE: No, it's gone quiet. I'll close the hatch.

THE DOCTOR: No, wait a minute. I'd better go down there.

VICTORIA: Oh no, no, not again!

THE DOCTOR: It's the only way to make sure.

JAMIE: Then I'll go with you.

THE DOCTOR: No wait . . . you stay and look after Victoria. I'll take somebody else.

(*He walks over to* TOBERMAN.)

THE DOCTOR: Toberman. You see what these creatures have done to you. They've tried to make you like them, do you understand?

(TOBERMAN *studies* THE DOCTOR's *face.*)

They've tried to make you their slave . . . they just want to use you.

(TOBERMAN *turns away to look at* KAFTAN.)

They are evil. Think of Kaftan.

TOBERMAN: Evil!

(*He clenches his fists.* JAMIE, VICTORIA *and* PARRY *are all round* THE DOCTOR *now. Behind them, unseen,* KLIEG *slowly rises to a sitting position. He looks round listening to their conversation.* TOBERMAN's *attention is wandering.*)

THE DOCTOR: They must be destroyed, do you see? Evil must be destroyed. Now come.

(TOBERMAN *nods and raises one of his powerful fists in anger.*)

TOBERMAN: Destroyed.

(THE DOCTOR *flinches slightly, then*

leads TOBERMAN *by the arm.*)

THE DOCTOR: Come on . . . come on.

> (TOBERMAN *hesitates. He turns.* KLIEG *lies down again pretending to be unconscious.* THE DOCTOR *goes to the hatch and climbs down, followed by* TOBERMAN.)

PARRY: Good luck.

THE DOCTOR: Thank you.

> (JAMIE *runs to the Cybergun and picks it up. He goes over to the hatch and calls down.*)

JAMIE: Doctor, the gun!

THE DOCTOR I shan't need that.

> (*He disappears from view.*)

JAMIE: He should've taken it.

> (CALLUM *groans in pain.*)

VICTORIA: Oh poor Mr. Callum. How are you feeling?

CALLUM: I can't move my arm . . .

> (JAMIE *goes over to join them. As soon as their backs are turned,* KLIEG *rises, seizes the Cybergun and quietly slips down the hatchway.*)

8. *THE CYBER TOMB*.

(*The Cybermen are in their cells. They are quite still, and their heads are bowed, but the membranes are not in position. The first signs of electric pulsing can be heard.*)

THE DOCTOR: Move quietly. They're all dormant, see.

(TOBERMAN *walks over to the conversion unit. He glares angrily at the apparatus, and strikes it with a tremendous blow. Part of it shatters.*)

TOBERMAN: Evil!

THE DOCTOR: No, quietly! They're only asleep. They're not frozen yet. Now . . . you watch them. I have things to do.

(*He goes over to the controls and studies them.*)

Now let me see, yes . . .

(THE DOCTOR *operates a switch, and a humming noise starts immediately.* KLIEG *enters unseen by either of them.*)

KLIEG: The cryostat, you're freezing them!

THE DOCTOR: Klieg!

(THE DOCTOR *moves towards* KLIEG. KLIEG *raises the Cybergun. He switches off the cryostat.*)

THE DOCTOR: No, no. You'll wake them up.

KLIEG: That is exactly my intention. You still don't understand, do you? Their Controller is dead, now I shall control them. They will do what I say.

(*His voice rings out in the tomb and one of the Cybermen stirs.*)

KLIEG: You see, Doctor. Yours is the privilege to witness for the first time the union between mass power and my absolute intelligence.

(KLIEG *looks round at* THE DOCTOR *and catches him trying to signal towards the doorway. As* KLIEG *turns,* JAMIE *darts out of sight.*)

Who is that . . . Come out.

(*There is no response.* KLIEG *turns his gun on* THE DOCTOR.)

Come out or I shall kill this man.

(JAMIE *comes out into the tomb.*)

Oh it's you! Over to that wall all of you. All of you! Now.

THE DOCTOR: Yes, as you say, such a combination between intelligence and power would make you formidable indeed. Why, you could be Commander of the Universe with your brilliance. It . . . it makes the imagination reel with the possibilities.

KLIEG: Why Doctor, if I had only known that you shared my imagination, you might even have worked for me.

THE DOCTOR: Perhaps it's not too late.

JAMIE: Doctor!

THE DOCTOR: No Jamie, don't you see? Don't you see what this is going to mean to all the people who come to serve Klieg the all-powerful? Why, no country, no person, would dare to have a single thought that was not your own. Eric Klieg's own conception of the other way of life.

(*The Cybermen's recovery is accelerating.*)

KLIEG: Brilliant! Yes, yes, you're right. Master of the World!

THE DOCTOR: Well, now I know you're mad. I just wanted to make sure.

(KLIEG *reacts as if he has been struck in the face. He jerks his gun at* THE DOCTOR.)

9. *THE CONTROL ROOM.*

(VICTORIA *and* PARRY *are listening nervously at the hatch.* HOPPER *enters.*)

HOPPER: Well, the fuel system's O.K. We can blast off any time.

VICTORIA: Sshhh!

PARRY: Oh, right.

HOPPER: Hey, what gives – where is everybody?

PARRY: Down there. And so are Klieg and the Cybermen.

HOPPER: Well, I hope they know what they're doing. I've been down there once and I don't reckon to go again.

VICTORIA: That's all right Captain. It's comforting to know that we have your superior strength to call on, should we need it.

10. *THE CYBER TOMB.*

KLIEG: And so, you have forfeited your right to survival. I shall make an example of you to all who question my intelligence and the supreme power of the Cybermen.

THE DOCTOR: You know I've heard this all before somewhere.

JAMIE: Hey, you know your trouble? You talk too much.

KLIEG: Oh, you're stupid. You still think that your puny minds can survive against us. You are decadent. Weak. Do you know that? Weak!

THE DOCTOR: All right, go ahead. Kill us!

KLIEG: No . . . I have a better idea, a much better idea. I shall leave you to the Cybermen. I am sure they will have some use for you . . . or parts of you.

(*He laughs maniacally.*)

Aaargh!

(*A Cyberman's arm whips around* KLIEG *and he is thrown to the ground, instantly dead. The Cyberman goes over to the control board.* JAMIE, TOBERMAN *and* THE DOCTOR *advance towards him. The Cyberman turns and faces them, raising both arms in attack.* TOBERMAN *struggles with the Cyberman.* THE DOCTOR *rushes over to the controls.* JAMIE *joins him.*)

THE DOCTOR: Quick. Jamie! These two levers – together!

JAMIE: I can't shift this one.

THE DOCTOR: What? You've got to trip that first.

(*Together, they slowly turn the wheel.* TOBERMAN *and the Cyberman struggle free from each other for a brief moment. Then they lock together, in a trial of strength. Slowly but surely, the Cyberman begins to gain the upper hand. Then suddenly* TOBERMAN *rips open the Cyberman's chest unit. Foam begins to gush from it.* THE DOCTOR *and* JAMIE *watch as the Cyberman slowly dies.* TOBERMAN *walks between* THE DOCTOR *and* JAMIE, *then goes off down the passageway.* THE DOCTOR *notices out of the corner of his eye that the tombs are beginning to freeze again.*)

THE DOCTOR: Last time they were frozen for five centuries. This time it must be forever!

(*He looks over the controls and makes sure of each one individually.*)

11. THE CONTROL ROOM.

(PARRY *is at the hatch.* TOBERMAN, HOPPER *and* VICTORIA *are standing by the hatch as* THE DOCTOR *and* JAMIE *emerge.*)

VICTORIA: Oh, Doctor!

THE DOCTOR: Here we are Victoria, safe and sound. Close the hatch.

JAMIE: All right.

(PARRY *operates the controls and the hatch begins to close.*)

There we are.

THE DOCTOR: Now then. Now the best thing about a machine that makes sense – you can very easily make it turn out nonsense. There we are. Now, I think you had better all go outside.

PARRY: Why? What are you going to do Doctor?

THE DOCTOR: I'm going to re-electrify the main doors – only this time, I am going to include the hatch and the control panel. Anyone touching any of them will get a considerable shock – in fact a fatal one.

PARRY: I see.

THE DOCTOR: Now, everyone outside. And please take him with you.

(*He indicates* PARRY.)

I shall be glad to see him outside.

VICTORIA: Jamie?

JAMIE: No, I'll stay with the Doctor.

VICTORIA: Oh all right.

(*As they leave, the* CYBER CONTROLLER *stirs and turns his head slightly.*)

THE DOCTOR: There we are, that's done.

(*Behind them the* CYBER CONTROLLER *rises shakily to his feet.*)

Now we just have to close the main doors and the circuit is complete.

JAMIE: Och, thank goodness for that.

(*He turns and sees the* CYBER CONTROLLER *blocking their way.*)

Doctor! Doctor!

(*The* CYBER CONTROLLER *takes a step forward, swaying slightly.*)

THE DOCTOR: Jamie . . . you go that way, I'll go this way. At least one of us will have a chance. When I say run . . . run!

(*They start to circle the* CYBER CONTROLLER *who looks round from one to the other.*)

Run!

(*They both run past him. He tries to catch first one, then the other, but he is moving too slowly, and they easily elude him. They run out of the doors.*)

12. THE TOMB ENTRANCE.

(THE DOCTOR *and* JAMIE *come out hurriedly and start swinging the huge doors closed.*)

THE DOCTOR: Quickly!

(*The door starts to shut.*)

Wait. Stop! We'll get a shock. We must find

something to insulate. I know, that shoring
timber over there. Hurry up . . . hurry up
. . . he's coming.

(JAMIE *brings some timber back to*
THE DOCTOR *and each seize a piece
and start to push the doors closed.*)

13. THE CONTROL ROOM.

(*The* CYBER CONTROLLER *slowly
lurches up to the doors which are now
nearly closed. He puts one huge hand
on each door and exerts his strength.
The doors stop closing.*)

14. THE TOMB ENTRANCE.

(THE DOCTOR *and* JAMIE *are exerting
all their strength, but the doors are
slowly being pushed open again.*)

THE DOCTOR: Oh, quickly . . . we must keep him inside,
else all our work will be wasted.

JAMIE: I can't hold mine. Come on.

THE DOCTOR: You must do!

(*The doors continue to move outwards.*
THE DOCTOR *and* JAMIE *are pushed
backwards and away. The* CYBER
CONTROLLER *is halfway through the
doors. Suddenly another pair of hands
join in –* TOBERMAN's.)

JAMIE: Toberman!

CONTROLLER: We – must – survive. We – must – survive.

TOBERMAN: You are evil.

THE DOCTOR: Toberman, come away.

JAMIE: Careful – you'll get killed man.

TOBERMAN: They shall never pass Toberman. The doors . . . close!

15. *THE CONTROL ROOM*

(*The doors close with a large flash. The* CYBER CONTROLLER *falls back, smoke gushing from his chest.*)

16. *THE TOMB ENTRANCE.*

(THE DOCTOR, JAMIE *and* PARRY *look back in horror.* TOBERMAN *is spread-eagled against the outside of the doors. He slowly slides down to the ground.*)

PARRY: How terrible – another life gone.

HOPPER: Come on Professor – blast off in nine minutes. Well, anybody coming along for the ride?

VICTORIA: We have our own . . . flying machine.

HOPPER: Flying machine?

VICTORIA: At least it works.

HOPPER: Oh, let's go.

PARRY: Right.

              (*He turns to* THE DOCTOR *and his friends.*)

              Well, goodbye Doctor.

THE DOCTOR: Goodbye.

PARRY: I'm sorry it had to end . . .

THE DOCTOR: I know . . . I know.

              (PARRY *moves off into the distance.*)

THE DOCTOR: Goodbye.

JAMIE: Now that really is the end of the Cybermen, isn't it?

THE DOCTOR: Yes Jamie. On the other hand . . . I never like to make predictions. Come along!

              (*As they walk away, we see a Cybermat on the ground, slowly moving . . .*)

On the back cover, Victor Pemberton is wrongly credited as 'script writer' for The Tomb of the Cybermen. *It should say 'script editor'.*